INTRODUCTION TO THE MYSTERY PLAYS
OF RUDOLF STEINER

INTRODUCTION
to the Mystery Plays of
Rudolf Steiner

EILEEN HUTCHINS

RUDOLF STEINER PRESS

Rudolf Steiner Press
Hillside House, The Square
Forest Row, RH18 5ES

E-mail: office@rudolfsteinerpress.com

www.rudolfsteinerpress.com

First published in Great Britain in 1984 by Rudolf Steiner Press
Reprinted 2014

© Rudolf Steiner Press 2014

All rights reserved. Apart from any fair dealing for the purpose of private study, research, criticism or review, as permitted under the Copyright, Designs and Patents Act, 1988, no part of this publication may be reproduced, stored in a retrieval system, or transmitted in any form or by any means, electronic, electrical, chemical, mechanical, optical, photocopying, recording or otherwise, without the prior written permission of the copyright owner. Inquiries should be addressed to the Publishers

A catalogue record for this book is available from the British Library

ISBN 978 1 85584 402 5

Cover by Morgan Creative featuring a photograph by David Macgregor
Typeset in Great Britain
Printed and bound by Beforts Ltd., Hertfordshire

CONTENTS

Acknowledgment

Foreword 1

The Portal of Initiation 3
(First Mystery Play)

The Soul's Probation 31
(Second Mystery Play)

The Guardian of the Threshold 62
(Third Mystery Play)

The Souls' Awakening 102
(Fourth Mystery Play)

Lectures by Rudolf Steiner useful as background 141
to the Mystery Dramas

Bibliography 142

ACKNOWLEDGMENT

I should like to express my thanks to the following friends who have given considerable help in the preparation and writing of this work: to Bert and Evelyn Capel, who asked me to undertake this task; to Paul M. Allen, especially for his willingness to discuss some of the leading themes; to Robina Pounder, for her patient and conscientious correcting and typing of the manuscript, and checking of the proofs; and to the many friends who read and made suggestions about certain passages.

Eileen M. Hutchins

AUTHOR'S FOREWORD

This introduction to Rudolf Steiner's Mystery Plays is not intended in any way to be an exhaustive explanation. It gives a series of suggestions and indications to help readers enter into the problems of the characters and the situations with which they are faced. Many students of Rudolf Steiner have been unable to make any connection with these dramas and, because of the long opening scene of the first play and the effort required to understand the different problems of all the leading characters, readers have tended to think the whole subject beyond them and so have given up the struggle. However the great importance of these plays is not that we are given many thoughts to further our understanding of anthroposophy but that we are shown the transforming power of spiritual striving in individual lives, and especially the development in human relationships through an awareness of the forces of destiny. In this respect the Mystery Plays are unique.

Once the reader is able to enter into the thoughts and relationships of the different characters these become alive and many of the problems are gradually solved. To explain every detail would have a stultifying effect, so much is left to the reader's awakening understanding.

When these dramas first appeared, Rudolf Steiner was presenting his spiritual insight from another angle than that of his previous teaching. Instead of addressing the awakened thinking through which anthroposophy can be understood as a path of knowledge, he was presenting in an artistic form the effect of a study of spiritual science on the lives of human beings. The first Mystery Play appeared in 1910, bringing a new impulse into the literary world of that time. At the beginning of this century there was a general demand for realistic drama as the only presentation of life that could be accepted as true. Although there were dramatists, such as Maeterlinck and Barrie,* who gave hints of a supersensible world, their themes appeared in the guise of fantasy. Any real knowledge beyond the sense perceptible was held to be out of the range of human attainment.

With regard to the first two dramas, *The Portal of Initiation* and *The Soul's Probation*, Rudolf Steiner does not claim that they are by him but through him, for in them he is drawing upon older spiritual traditions. He describes the first as a Rosicrucian drama. Here on the one hand he is following certain teachings developed in true Rosicrucianism, on the other he acknowledges his debt to Goethe, describing his Mystery Play as a development of Goethe's story, *The Green Snake and the Beautiful Lily*. In this fairy tale is represented the longing of those involved in the sense world to attain an understanding of the spirit of which the material realm is an image. Owing to his supersensible perceptions Goethe was able to give a minute reflection of true spiritual events. Rudolf Steiner develops the same theme though with a different approach, representing human beings in their striving within the tensions of present-day life.

In the second drama, *The Soul's Probation*, he draws upon traditions of the teaching of the Knights Templar. But in the third and fourth plays, Rudolf Steiner proclaims that they are by him as they represent the working of anthroposophy in individual lives and for this he takes personal responsibility.

*Strindberg, another such dramatist, could now be added, but he was then hardly known beyond Sweden.

THE PORTAL OF INITIATION

The Prologue
The first drama is introduced by a Prologue. At first sight this seems to have little bearing on the theme of the play itself. But on serious consideration we find that it forms an integral part of the whole structure. We are introduced to two friends who discuss what the true nature of art should be; and we see here how Rudolf Steiner is preparing us to understand a drama which is in every way vastly different from contemporary plays. He is revealing the sources from which true art should spring.

As the scene opens Sophia is practising a song with her two children. The words which seem so simple are in a way the opening note of the play itself for they express the uplifting of man's being through wonder and gratitude to the creative spirits of the world. This theme is developed and transformed during the course of the drama.

Estella now enters. She has come hoping to persuade Sophia to accompany her to the performance of a play *Entebrten des Leibes und der Seele*, translated by Ruth and Hans Pusch as *The Uprooted* but rather more accurately by Harry Collison as *Outcasts from Body and from Soul*. She has failed to remember that the Group to which Sophia belongs is also producing a drama which they have been rehearsing for a long time.

Estella is disturbed as she feels that Sophia is drawing away from her and losing touch with everyday life. She herself considers it necessary to face up to grim realities and not to console oneself with abstract ideals. Sophia points out that her friend is considering human beings only as the products of the conditions into which they have been born, whereas in reality, through a living thinking, it is possible for one to transform one's surroundings. Members of her Group do not wish to inculcate abstract ideals but to present ideas, which, through a creative germinating force, can awaken new powers. The mere representation of human misery cannot comfort those who sorrow nor give strength to those who toil. In concentrating solely on misfortune we fail to recognise what is creative in human relationships. Estella cannot follow Sophia's line of thought and considers that she is indulging in fantasy. Although she wants to remain friends, Estella expresses her great disappointment that Sophia will not fit in with her plans.

We learn later that the theme of *The Uprooted* is the same as that of the first Mystery Drama itself but whereas the former, in representing certain human problems and difficulties from an entirely materialistic point of view, cannot indicate any solution, the *Portal of Initiation* shows that, through the development of higher faculties, suffering can be transcended.

Scene One
The scene opens in the sittingroom adjoining a hall where a lecture on anthroposophy has just been delivered. At the rear and to the left is a bust of Ahriman as a sign that in our daily life we are in his realm. The left of the stage is the receiving side so that Ahriman is a listener. It is only in the fourth play that he becomes fully active and walks across the stage in the background. It is of great importance that spiritual knowledge is cultivated just where his influence is likely to be most active.

During the opening scene all the leading characters make

their appearance and give their impressions of the lecture. We learn from them their views of life and hear of their special difficulties. The first to appear are the two main actors in the drama. Maria, a devoted student of the lecturer Benedictus, is hostess in the house where the lecture has taken place. Johannes, a young artist, who has been drawn into her circle, has received inspiration and joy from her teaching. But he is now at a critical turning point in his career. He has come to realise that all he has learnt from her has dulled his own natural genius so that he is no longer able to create. What has given Maria joyous confidence in spiritual knowledge has led him into darkness and despair. This arouses in Maria doubts about her own leadership when what has brought enlightenment to her, has turned to its opposite in him.

At this moment other characters enter upon the scene. Philia, Astrid and Luna have a special relationship with Maria. They are here introduced as human beings, but in later scenes, where supersensible worlds are represented, they appear as the soul powers of Maria. They are followed by two characters who play leading parts in the later dramas. Professor Capesius and Doctor Strader are typical intellectual thinkers at the beginning of this century. Capesius, who, according to Rudolf Steiner's comments to Hans Pusch, is between 50 and 55 years of age, has made his career the teaching of history. He has been specially interested in following up the changing characteristics of different epochs of civilisation. But he has come to the conclusion that, however interesting these studies may be, thoughts are only shadowy reflections of reality and have not the power to shape events. Yet he has been impressed by the lecturer's claim that words can penetrate into the sphere of will and give strength for the tasks of life.

Strader is a scientist for whom life has been a hard struggle. He tells how he grew up among simple pious people and in his youth wished to become a monk; but, after contacting modern scientific thinking, he came to doubt all religious teaching and could no longer enter the church. As he now considers that the only faculty by which man can judge is that of reason, he has found the lecture convincing. Only facts confirmed by scientific research can give him a firm ground of support.

After the conversation between Capesius and Strader however, an incident occurs which has far-reaching effects. Theodora appears on the scene. She has recently joined Maria's group, but differs from the others in that from time to time she has visionary experiences. She now suddenly passes into a trance-like condition and speaks of a vision which appears before her. She beholds a radiant figure who announces Himself as the Christ, who once lived on earth in bodily form, but will now appear to those who are able to experience Him as a spiritual Being. We know from Rudolf Steiner that this power will be attained by a number of people during this century, especially from the year 1935 onwards. Theodora has acquired this gift. It might appear that she is a seeress possessed of old atavistic perceptions; but it seems to me that this is not necessarily the case. Her character during the subsequent plays shows a poise and wisdom one does not associate with atavistic powers. It is true that her spiritual knowledge is not acquired in the same way as that of Maria, who has striven and disciplined herself to attain her present stature; nevertheless, Theodora reveals a state of consciousness that will gradually be manifested more and more widely as the century progresses.

Theodora's announcement has a remarkable effect upon

Strader. Capesius is inclined to regard her words as only a reflection of what she has heard from Benedictus; but Strader considers her revelation as a psychic phenomenon which has to be taken into account. This event is actually the beginning of his awakening to the validity of other powers than mere reason.

At this moment other characters enter. Felix Balde and his wife Felicia have come on a long journey to be present at the gathering. They live in a remote place in the mountains and from one year's end to another meet hardly a single soul. Because of their solitude and the beauty of their surroundings they have acquired unique gifts. We learn that Benedictus seeks them out to have conversations with Felix, and Capesius visits them from time to time. He now confesses that he often experiences moments in his life when he feels empty and exhausted. At such times he makes his way to Felicia, who tells him folk tales full of an ancient wisdom through which new life flows into his whole being. But on the other hand he regards Felix as an eccentric who talks unintelligible jargon about nature beings and demons. Benedictus draws attention to the fact that anyone who listens thoughtfully will realise that powers of nature are striving to manifest themselves through Felix's words. In fact his methods of expression can be compared with the writings of Jacob Boehme which were also unintelligible to those who lacked understanding of the realms he described.

After Felix, Felicia and Benedictus have taken their departure, Strader expresses great anxiety. The seeress's vision has shattered him and he has a foreboding of dark days ahead. He confesses to Capesius that he sometimes has a strange experience. When puzzled by unsolved riddles, he becomes aware of a dream-like being rising out of the darkness to mock him and to warn him that unless he can overcome it with his dull thinking power, he is only a phantom of his own delusions. Capesius has little understanding of Strader's condition and warns him that if he allows himself to lose his certainty of mind he will begin to doubt everything.

Another group now appears. We meet with certain figures who on the one hand represent religious traditions of the past but on the other are typical of modern attitudes. Theodosius is the follower of religious teachings which have become traditional and sentimental. Romanus, who has especially developed the forces of the will, expresses views which are similar to those of Marxists. He considers that only activity in practical work can forward human progress. Gairman (Germanus in the original) is the typical modern cynic who loves to mock at everything serious. Yet he has been deeply impressed by the lecture and realises that an unseen power has laid hold of him which is stronger than the thin house of cards built up by his mocking wit. A man of this century who can be compared to Gairman is Bernard Shaw, who on the one hand has revealed a longing for a certain idealism, yet has shown a horror of sentimentality, and so with his intellect has been quick to expose the flaws in any idealistic philosophy. This is especially apparent in *Saint Joan*.

Together with these three we meet the Other Maria. She is so named because of her very close relationship with the leading character of the play. But whereas Maria's acceptance of Benedictus's teaching and her connection with others are guided by the light of her conscious intelligence, the Other Maria acts out of warmth of heart; but her life experiences have taught her that this alone is not enough. Through the heavy burdens she had to bear throughout her life, she became utterly exhausted until she met with Maria's group. She found among them a teaching which brought her the light of understanding. She now describes to those around her how words of power gave her new strength.

After the departure of the visitors Maria and Johannes are left alone and we hear of the impression made upon him by all that has taken place. As an artist he has the ability to enter into the thoughts and feelings of all around him and this has given him the shattering experience that he himself has no separate existence but is only the reflection of his surroundings. This liberation from his own narrow egoism has made him aware of his own limitations and failures. He tells Maria how in joining her circle he deserted a young girl who loved him. Until recently he viewed the whole event light-heartedly, but now suddenly he is shaken by a realisation of his guilt and feels responsible for her death. Maria, sympathising with his desperate grief, tells him that there is only one who can now help him and that is their leader Benedictus.

At this moment she is called away and a woman, who has not hitherto appeared, draws near to Johannes. Helena is a representative of Luciferic powers. She tells Johannes that knowledge of the spirit can bring only bliss and his grief and despondency are due to lack of true spiritual wisdom. In reality Johannes has made a step forward in his development through recognising his own faults. In this first stage of enlightenment he is able to realise Helena's injunctions as a temptation and to reject her facile optimism.

Scene Two
A LANDSCAPE OF ROCKS AND SPRINGS representing Johannes' inner experiences. This is actually a presentation

of what is going on in the soul of Johannes during the previous scene.

Here we take part in Johannes' imaginative vision. His participation in the thoughts and feelings of the characters in Maria's group and his awakening to the evil within himself have brought him supersensible experiences. He is aware that the whole world of Nature is summoning him to self-knowledge. He hears the springs and rocks calling to him: 'O man, know thou thyself'.

Then occurs the event which Rudolf Steiner describes as the meeting with the Guardian of the Threshold. Johannes is aware that he is facing a dark abyss. He is separated from his bodily shell and his lower being appears to him as a raging dragon begot of lust and greed. He has an experience similar to that endured by the soul after death. It seems to him that the young girl of whose death he feels guilty, is speaking through him and he has to feel within himself the pain he inflicted. Self-knowledge has enabled him to pour himself into another being. He now knows that he is fettered to the pernicious monster who is his own lower self.

At this moment Maria appears before him, drawn by her own awareness of his suffering. She feels unable to help him herself but directs him to Benedictus. She confesses that she also is in deep trouble. She can no longer bear the riddle of her life, for she now has to face the fact that whenever she brings to those connected with her the light of her spiritual wisdom, it seems to work destructively upon them. She is sure that Johannes' sufferings are part of the thorny path which is to lead him to the truth and that he is called upon to live through each terror. She knows that the light they seek may be darkened but can never be extinguished. However, in their present difficulties they both need help.

We can compare her situation here with that of the Lily in Goethe's fairy tale.

Scene Three
A ROOM FOR MEDITATION
Johannes and Maria have come to Benedictus. Maria first asks guidance for a child she has adopted. Benedictus gives the child words to be pondered before he goes to sleep: 'The heavenly powers of light are carrying me into the spirit's house'. We have here a variation on one of the leading motifs of the drama which first appears in the Prologue.

When the child has left, Maria tells of his background. He had been deserted in infancy and Maria had taken him into her care. With the help of Benedictus she had guided him so that his natural gifts had unfolded most beautifully but he had never shown any particular affection for his foster mother. However one day, observing a trance of Theodora, he rushed in fright to Maria for protection and from that moment love for her was awakened. But at the same time his inborn gifts began to decline. Maria now appeals to Benedictus to solve her life's enigma.

There now follows one of the most difficult passages in the whole series of plays. Benedictus explains that Maria's sorrow is part of a knot of destiny spun by karma in world becoming, as the deeds of gods now need to unite with the lives of human beings. He describes how he himself had been approached by spirit powers to select a human soul as a worthy messenger of divine worlds, for a turning point in time is now demanding an important step forward in evolution. His gaze fell upon Maria as one whose life had fitted her to become a mediator bearing new healing powers. However her task to ripen spirit faculties in others required that she should destroy qualities which are only of temporary worth, as the sacrifice of the temporal quickens immortal seeds. Hence in her relationship with others she has had to destroy what is of no eternal value.

This revelation makes such a powerful impression upon Maria that her soul leaves her physical body and she appears to lose consciousness. Now Johannes has to face a terrible ordeal. From her lips emerge the most bitter curses. She declares that the light given by Benedictus has revealed that she is only a spirit's mediator and not her true self. She curses him for making her the tool of 'evil hellish beings'. One instant has shown her that he is not the great leader she imagined. He has misled her in order to mislead others and her love for him is changed into wild hatred.

Johannes realises that he is not listening to his friend but to some gruesome fiend. Benedictus explains that, as the real being of Maria has left her body, the enemy of good has been able to take possession of it in order to destroy Benedictus' work. Because true spirits have often spoken to Johannes through Maria's lips, world-destiny has not spared him from hearing the evil utterances of the prince of hell. Maria's true being is soaring in spirit heights where Johannes will now be able to follow her to the Temple of the Sun. Benedictus reveals the cause of Johannes' sufferings which are due to a knot in the threads of karma through which he has been called to wrest his way in order to develop new powers. As he has stood firm through this terrible trial, Benedictus is now able to see his star shining in full radiance. From the moment he despaired of himself and yet wrestled on, he acquired a wisdom greater than the faith he had previously been granted. He has now proved himself a true pupil of Benedictus, mature enough to follow Maria to spirit heights.

THE PORTAL OF INITIATION 13

This episode arouses great problems for many readers. If so highly developed a being as Maria can become the vessel of evil powers, how can we be sure that other spiritual leaders are not liable to be possessed in a similar way? Might not any revered guide likewise become the mouthpiece of evil beings? A natural healthy judgement resists such a thought.

In answer to this we can consider two facts. The first is that the scene takes place in the presence of Benedictus who through his understanding is able to control the situation. The second is that the event is connected with a karmic knot in which Maria and Johannes have become entangled. Light is not thrown on this particular situation until the fourth drama when it is revealed that in a far distant incarnation Maria failed to achieve initiation on account of her connection with Johannes.

As Johannes has proved himself victorious in this test, Benedictus is now able to give him a meditation to provide him with a key to the spiritual worlds.

> Light's weaving essence radiates
> through far-flung spaces
> to fill the world with life.
> Love's blessing pours its warmth
> through time's long ages
> to call forth revelation of all worlds.
> And messengers of spirit join
> light's weaving essence
> with revelation of the soul.
> And when with both the human being
> can join his own true self,
> he is alive in spirit heights.

In the Prologue the quality of the light is expressed in a

simple song, arousing the singing of the birds, calling the plants to life and awakening in the hearts of men gratitude to the spirits of the world. These thoughts and feelings are now more fully developed in the given meditation. We are made aware of the beings who live and work in light and warmth and who pour their love and blessing down to earth so that spirit messengers can unite with them to awaken a response in human souls.

Through this guidance Johannes is able to pass beyond the confused experiences that had worked so devastatingly upon him and enter the different supersensible realms without losing his way.

Scene Four
A LANDSCAPE REPRESENTING THE SOUL WORLD
We now follow Johannes into the Elemental World where his first meeting is with the two kinds of evil that threaten mankind. Lucifer is the Tempter who would lure man away from his earthly tasks into a spiritual realm for which he is not yet prepared. Ahriman, referred to in the Gospels as Satan, would lead man to deny the spirit and concentrate on the material world. Lucifer claims that it is he who has given Johannes his freedom and he promises him the joy of selfhood. Ahriman on the other hand declares that he has led man out of spirit darkness to find truth in the world of the senses. When Johannes recognises their deceptive lures, they disappear.

Johannes is now aware of the Spirit of the Elements, the Being who guides the incarnating soul into earthly life, and the sleeping soul back into the physical world. We are here in the realm which human beings pass through in sleep, where they have to live in reverse their life of the preceding day and witness its effect on the Elemental World.

The Spirit of the Elements is here guiding the souls of Capesius and Strader to the surface of the earth. But as these two have little understanding of the supersensible, their presence causes him much pain, and he complains that their earth-bound thoughts create raging storms in his kingdom.

Although in earthly life Capesius is the older, he here appears to Johannes as a young man who responds to his surroundings with feelings of euphoria. He imagines that he will be able to bring back into earthly life inspirations awakened by what he is here experiencing; but his boastful words are met with thunder and lightning.

Strader, on the other hand, who is still relatively young, appears here in old age. He is a seeker after truth and to him it seems that appearances in the Elemental World are illusory. The Spirit of the Elements warns them both that they are ignorant of the sources of thought and life.

Strader is reminded of the terrifying dream-like being who from time to time rises into his consciousness to warn him of the powerlessness of his own dull thinking; but he tries to defy the Spirit of the Elements. The Spirit now demands his reward for having given them both their selfhood. Capesius' offer to pay him in thoughts and words inspired by his present experiences, is rejected and the Spirit demands that as they can give nothing they must ask for payment from the woman who has endowed their souls with power. He then disappears.

We are made aware that some response is required from human beings in return for the gifts bestowed on them by the spirit world, and the one who has led souls into a relationship with the spirit has to take responsibility for their shortcomings. We are reminded of the incident in Goethe's tale where the wife of the Old Man with the Lamp incurs a debt on behalf of the Will of the Wisps.

Capesius and Strader do not know how to proceed. Capesius feels that progress can be made only by giving expression to their own inner impulses; but Strader considers that they must have in view what is of benefit to all mankind.

At this moment Johannes becomes aware of the Other Maria. She appears in radiant beauty, as through her warmth of love she is able to bring to expression the creative powers of Nature. She resembles the Green Snake of Goethe's tale, who through sacrifice transforms what she has absorbed from the sense world into shining jewels that create the bridge between the world of the senses and the world of the spirit.

Capesius and Strader seek her help, but she warns them that unless they can find their way back to everyday earthly life, it will never go well with them. The abstract thinking of today estranges man from a sense of reality. The Other Maria indicates two ways by which they might proceed. One would appear to be the Goethean approach to a living understanding of all manifestations of nature; the other a return to the innocent wonder and reverence of childhood. We may say that the one is illustrated in the Gospel of St. Matthew and the other in that of St. Luke. She disappears and Capesius comments, 'Then after all we are thrown back upon ourselves'. Neither of them yet has any ability to understand the realm into which they have been led.

Just as most of those who awake from sleep have no recollection of what they have experienced during the night, so Capesius and Strader can bring back nothing consciously into their earthly life. However, Johannes is aware of what he has seen although he is not sure of its reality.

Scene Five
THE HIDDEN MYSTERY CENTRE OF THE
HIEROPHANTS

In this scene Johannes is able to perceive in imaginative vision an underground temple representing the esoteric wisdom of the Mystery Centres. Here four hierophants stand each behind his altar. We are reminded of the temple in Goethe's fairy tale where three kings of gold, silver and copper represent the powers of thinking, feeling and willing; and where the fourth, the mixed king, is an expression of the confused faculties of so many modern leaders where thoughts are dictated by prejudice and where deeds are so often the result of outworn religious and social traditions.

Benedictus, as the one who is to bring a new dawn, through the awakening of an individual living thinking, takes his place in the east. Theodosius, who is inspired by the warmth of feeling, is in the south. Romanus, exponent of the forces of materialism, is in the west. And Retardus, representative of the mixed king, who has not previously appeared, is in the north, the region of frost and death.

Benedictus alone appears in full ego-consciousness for he is to bring esoteric knowledge into the light of day. Theodosius and Romanus serve the world powers of feeling and will, quite apart from their activities in everyday life. In fact as human beings they appeared in the first scene as one-sided and limited in outlook; nevertheless spiritual forces are able to work through them.

Benedictus has been able to lead Johannes through the first stages of his pupilship but cannot give him the assurance of the truth of his visions without the help of Theodosius and Romanus, because his own teaching springs from himself alone whereas they allow cosmic spirits to speak through them. We see here how in developing spiritual consciousness the bearer of a new impulse draws strength from those who have nurtured the esoteric wisdom of the past.

Now that Johannes has become free from the fetters of his sense impressions, Theodosius is able to inspire him with the warmth of love so that he will be able to hear the speech of the spiritual world. Romanus gives him the power to act creatively. However Retardus, who opposes any new birth, considers that mankind is not yet ready for enlightenment and that the earth has given no sign of needing new initiates. He states that faith should still be the guide for mankind in general and higher knowledge must remain the secret wisdom of those who have received special preparation.

At the moment when Romanus affirms that human beings who have not been initiated are now drawing near out of their own impulses, Felix Balde and the Other Maria enter the temple. Felix proclaims that the earth is in dire distress as men with their intellectual thinking can no longer nourish it. They affirm that the world has come into being from a purely material origin. When he describes its spiritual nature, he is regarded as a dreamer or a fool and no one will listen to him. The Other Maria speaks of how in the past she acted out of her own resources of love, but she now realises that by uniting with the leaders of the temple, her work and that of Felix will be furthered.

Benedictus confirms that with their help the consecration of Johannes can be completed. Theodosius and Romanus announce that the newcomers' union with the powers of the temple will bring warmth of love and strength for action to those who seek the spirit.

Retardus alone stands in opposition. When the wisdom, which has hitherto been guarded in secret, becomes open to those who have not been initiated according to the old methods, his own power will no longer avail. Benedictus instructs him that he needs to transform himself as his former way of working is no longer effective.

In his vision Johannes recognises the characters he met after the lecture; but, as we learn from the seventh scene yet to come, he is still unsure whether what he beholds is dream or reality.

Scene Six
A LANDSCAPE REPRESENTING THE SOUL WORLD
(as in Scene Four)
Johannes now becomes aware of the burden of responsibility undertaken by one who has aided other human beings along the path to spiritual knowledge.

Felicia Balde has brought the wisdom expressed in her fairy tales to Capesius and Strader, and, though they have not understood their deeper meaning, they have been refreshed by powers more life-giving than their limited intellectualism. But such a gift cannot be bestowed without sacrifice. The Spirit of the Elements summons her to make restitution for their lack of understanding which has caused storms in the supersensible world. He warns her that the etheric forces which she has poured forth will cause ugliness in her own physical body. This arouses Felicia's indignation as she protests that these two have already ruined her young son. He had been brought up by Felix and herself with open-hearted devotion to all that they had given him through their wisdom. But these men had led him astray by fascinating him with their arid materialistic thought. The Spirit assures her that when new powers have been awakened in the souls of men, her maternal beauty and her child's gifts will blossom more fully.

He now orders her to pay him by creating a fairy tale which will inspire the spirits of the rocks to help him in his work. We are now made aware that what is living in language has its effect not only in the physical but also in the supersensible world. The beings of nature require the co-operation of man.

Rudolf Steiner warned Collison not to add any fancy interpretations to Felicia's story and added that she herself did not fully understand its true content. But we can live more fully into its meaning by pondering the meditation given by Benedictus at the end of the third scene when Johannes has survived his stern trial. He speaks the words:

> messengers of spirit join
> light's weaving essence
> with revelations of the soul.

In Felicia's tale we hear how a Being of the Sun leaves for one night his journey round the world to comfort a man who has grown old and weary wrestling with the problems of human love and hate. When the Being rejoins the Sun in its round and returns once more, the old man has died. He has been freed from his struggle.

Gairman, the representative of the earthly intellect, now appears on the scene to mock at Felicia's tale by giving a caricature of her theme. He tells of a dry researcher who has sought to record in statistics examples in life of love and hate. He finds that they appear to balance out. When however he meets the Beings of Love and Hate he is deaf to their utterances. Gairman rightly expresses the experience of a dry materialist, but this is painful to Felicia who seeks a true understanding of spirit beings and their relationship to man. However, Gairman is anxious to make himself heard more widely than to human beings, who pay little attention to him.

Scene Seven
THE REALM OF SPIRIT
At this point the first theme of the drama comes to its fulfilment. We are now in the spirit realm where Maria and Johannes discover their true spiritual relationship.

Maria is calling on her three soul powers to assist her in raising Johannes to true existence. The brothers in the temple have held council and call on her to arouse in him the strength for spirit flight. Philia, Astrid and Luna no longer appear as human beings but are the powers of Maria's own soul. It is impossible to give the content of their conversation in simple words, we can only live into their mood and allow them to vibrate in our own being. Philia is more connected with the feeling life or sentient soul, Astrid with the thinking or intellectual soul and Luna with the will life or consciousness soul of Maria. She is confident that with their help she will succeed in her task. She now hears the call of Johannes who is finding his way into their world of light.

Johannes describes how he has been freed from the bonds of sense and has seen different aspects of Capesius and Strader from the way they appear on earth. Capesius, who is advanced in years, has appeared as a young man, while the more youthful Strader has seemed more elderly. Only those who are filled with spirit appear to his vision as they are in earthly life. He is aware that the brothers in the temple have shown their favour, but only now that he beholds Maria in her true spiritual being is he assured that he has grasped reality.

Theodora, who has been near at hand together with

Maria's adopted child, is now able to enlighten Maria and Johannes about their karmic relationship. In the light that shines above Maria's head, she sees in vision a picture of olden times. She recognises Maria as she was in a past incarnation, when from the Hibernian Mysteries she brought the teaching of Christ to heathen tribes. At first they received the message with anger, but gradually the calm radiance of the priest convinced them. Only one continued to threaten vengeance. This soul is now incarnated in the child at Theodora's side. A woman in the crowd listened to the new revelation and fell in devotion before the priest. In this figure Johannes now recognises himself.

Maria is able to show him that the pain and doubt they both endured was owing to this early relationship which worked so strongly in them both but was unrecognised. But the suffering itself gave them the power to win entry into spirit realms. As through all his trials Johannes remained faithful to her, she can now bring his consecration in the spirit land to completion for he is assured of the reality of his supersensible experiences. He has needed to meet in the spirit someone with whom he has been deeply connected in earthly life.

We now receive the reverse picture of what appeared to happen in the third scene when Johannes had to witness Maria's apparent cursing of Benedictus. She here speaks of how on that occasion Benedictus solved for her the riddle of her life and how he had called her to the service of the Spirit who sought to guide human evolution by alliance with an earthly being.

Now that Johannes has succeeded in discovering his true relationship with Maria, Benedictus is able to give him a further mantram. This is a transformed version of the one that appears at the end of Scene Three. We again hear of the blessings bestowed from the spiritual world by Light and Love, but attention is now paid to the way in which these are received by man. It is all important that through understanding and love human beings should be able to create together and perform spiritual acts in return for the gifts they have received from the Divine.

The four Mystery Plays illustrate how individual human beings have to help one another so that they can make progress in spiritual knowledge and learn to bring about a new state of consciousness.

Interlude

Now that Maria and Johannes have achieved knowledge of their true relationship, we return to Sophia and Estella. Both have been witnessing a drama, and we are now given the impression that it is Sophia's group who has presented the scenes we have here been considering.

From the opening conversation it becomes clear that Estella has no interest in Sophia's activities but is anxious only to pour out her own feelings and win her friend's sympathy. The realistic drama which she has seen has presented the same theme as that of Maria's company, but from an entirely external viewpoint; hence the young artist, unable to win the sensual love of his benefactress, and haunted by the death of the young girl he has deserted, falls into utter despair and his life becomes a complete ruin.

Though Sophia sympathises with Estella who has been deeply moved by this tragedy, she tries to point out that it is not the task of art to imitate life, as an imitation is less powerful than the creations of Nature, who has given man the urge to continue the creative process; and his revealing of what lies hidden behind the outer appearances of life is what gives inspiration to art.

Estella is unable to understand this line of thought and reproaches her friend for not sharing her feelings. But Sophia points out the necessity of their accepting what life has to bring.

Scene Eight
Maria is watching Johannes, intent on completing a portrait of Capesius. We learn that three years have passed since the events related in Scene Seven. Capesius is describing how he met Johannes for the first time at the lecture given in Maria's house and how he was then struck by the young artist's expression of extreme sorrow so that he appeared absolutely unaware of anything but his own misery. Yet it seemed that through his grief he was absorbing all that occurred around him. Then a little later, to Capesius' great surprise, he found Johannes completely changed. His whole being expressed confidence and joy.

Soon after this Johannes came and asked to be Capesius' pupil. A close friendship grew up which led to his undertaking to paint the historian's portrait. The latter was astonished at the development in Johannes' art, for he now seemed able to reveal what was hidden from the world of the senses. Capesius himself never doubted that there were worlds inaccessible to our normal range of understanding, but he had not felt confident enough to try to bring these to expression.

During Capesius' description of Johannes' art, Strader enters. He complains that he does not understand Capesius, for surely spirit expresses itself in every work of art. Capesius points out that the artist is generally unaware of what inspires him, whereas Johannes is conscious of what he perceives in the spirit.

During this conversation Strader speaks of Johannes

by his second name of Thomasius and Capesius takes this up, perhaps as an indication of Johannes' change of consciousness. However, throughout the rest of the play the name Johannes is retained.

Strader is deeply troubled as he has to acknowledge that Johannes has certainly been able to reveal aspects of Capesius that he himself has never before realised. Yet he cannot believe in conscious spirit sight, for he considers that the artist creates out of innate powers similar to those that bring the plants to life. He cannot understand how forms and colours can express what lives in Capesius' inner being. It is as though Johannes were conjuring up ghosts.

Capesius encourages Strader to believe that this is an important turning point for him. He claims that Johannes has the power to penetrate beyond the illusion of the senses to knowledge of the spirit-self. Maria adds that it is necessary to transform oneself in order truly to know oneself, and hence knowledge differs at each stage of life.

This is more than Strader can bear as it implies the limitations of reason and he rushes out in distress, followed by Capesius. Maria comments that Capesius is closer to spirit knowledge than he realises and Strader suffers deeply because he cannot find what he longs for so earnestly.

Johannes now reveals what he has been able to read in Capesius' inner being. He has recognised certain powers acquired during a previous life which cannot come to expression in this incarnation. He has not been able to penetrate to Capesius' past lives but has recognised his present depth of soul and has thus been able to unveil for him his inmost self.

The scene closes with Maria's comment that what has been revealed will work on further in Capesius' inner being.

Scene Nine
A LANDSCAPE OF ROCKS AND SPRINGS
(as in Scene Two)
Here we have a transformation of Johannes' experiences in the second scene. He is once more aware that Nature calls him to develop his own powers, but he has risen beyond the sight of his lower self which caused him so much horror and has won confidence in the forces of growth within his own being. Hence he has an imaginative vision of the radiant spirit heights to which he will ultimately attain. He will thus gain strength to bring relief to the soul of the young girl he wronged. His horror has been changed into an impulse to redeem.

Although Johannes has not yet passed the Guardian of the Threshold and is still liable to fall into illusions, he is nevertheless filled with hope and the urge to reach the heights he can foresee. Again he is able to call Maria into communion with his own being and she beholds his star shining in its full power.

Scene Ten
A ROOM FOR MEDITATION
We here become aware of the struggles Johannes has to endure before he can attain spirit certainty. In meditation, the being of Theodosius appears to him and Johannes is filled with creative joy. He imagines he will be able to express through his art the inspiration Theodosius is able to give him. Theodosius disappears but Johannes is convinced that his revelations will continue.

However, his euphoria is followed by a feeling that evil powers are approaching him and he must strengthen himself to meet the fiercest of adversaries.

To his astonishment Benedictus appears before him and

he is thrown into confusion. He calls upon the good forces of his soul to shatter the illusion. Benedictus speaks warning words. Johannes needs to remember what he owes to Benedictus who has enabled the fruit of wisdom to grow within him. He can now progress only if he allows wisdom's light to shine forth from the Temple where Benedictus works together with his brothers.

Johannes feels strengthened, but Theodosius again appears in the guise of a tempter, for Lucifer is working through him. Johannes once more feels inspired and he calls to the spirit within himself to come forth from concealment. Immediately Lucifer appears, for it is he who works within the being of man who has not attained full illumination. Lucifer is then followed by Ahriman who calls to Johannes not to allow himself to be dissolved in cosmic heights.

We need remember that these two beings now speak in different words from those used in Scene Four when they were appealing to his lower ego. Lucifer calls:

> O man know me,
> O man sense yourself.

While Ahriman declares:

> O man sense me,
> O man know thyself.

Johannes is now a stage further in self-knowledge, but he is still open to illusions. It is important for him to achieve a balance between the influences of these two powers and not fall a prey to them in his path of progress.

Scene Eleven
THE SUN TEMPLE: THE HIDDEN MYSTERY CENTRE OF THE HIEROPHANTS

(Now at the surface of the earth)

The Mystery Centre of the Hierophants is no longer concealed in the darkness of the earth but has come forth into the light of day. This is Johannes' prophetic vision of the future. We can see from the previous two scenes that he is not yet fully mature and we learn in the succeeding dramas how many struggles he will have to encounter before acquiring 'spirit peacefulness of soul'.

When the scene opens, Retardus is reproaching Capesius and Strader because they have not remained true to his teaching. He complains that he inspired Capesius with lofty ideals and gave him the gift of eloquence. He then led him into Maria's and Johannes' circle so that he might draw them away from their interest in spiritual pursuits. But instead of fulfilling his wishes, Capesius fell under their spell. On the other hand, he had called upon Strader to destroy the power of spirit vision, but he had fallen a prey to doubt. Thus through them Maria and Johannes are lost to Retardus' realm.

They are able to plead that the views with which Retardus has inspired them are unable to satisfy the deepest impulses of the human heart.

Benedictus appears with Lucifer and Ahriman. We here see them in their rightful spheres. Lucifer, when recognised, can inspire human beings with a love of beauty, but can no longer dominate men's souls. Ahriman can introduce those who approach him to the true value of the material world, but cannot chain the ones who have attained spiritual vision to a belief in its ultimate truth.

The leading characters in the drama now make their

appearance. We are shown how much they are dependent on one another, and are reminded of the words of the Old Man with the Lamp in Goethe's tale: 'One alone can do but little, but he can avail who in the proper hour unites his strength with others'.

Theodosius makes it clear that Maria, who has attained the light of love, cannot fulfil her task of guiding Johannes without the support of the Other Maria's warmth which has hitherto remained without conscious direction. The Other Maria acknowledges that warmth of feeling is not enough and she will no longer deprive love of the radiance of understanding.

Johannes is also dependent on the Other Maria's enlightenment. However, his guide Maria warns him that he has attained spirit knowledge through her, but he will come to understand the true nature of the soul only when he recognises his own inmost being as he has recognised hers. Philia, Astrid and Luna, who once more appear as the soul powers of Maria, indicate to Johannes the different realms of soul he will need to experience; the joy of feeling, the light of living thinking and the consciousness of the true self.

Romanus requires the support of Felix Balde who has hitherto failed to ally himself with the leaders of the Temple because he has not felt the need to work with others. Felix confesses that it is the folly of men in their complete misunderstanding of the earth that has shown him the necessity of uniting with the Hierophants. His approach enables Romanus to enlighten the wills of Maria and Johannes. Johannes realises that he can now be strengthened, through the act which has brought Felix to the Temple, to find his own way into the temple of the soul.

Retardus complains that Maria and Johannes have torn

themselves away from his leadership. But Felicia is able to show that as long as human beings can awaken within themselves the fire of thought they do not need his help, and she is able to give a knowledge that will bear fruit. Benedictus confirms that Capesius has also set forth on the path to freedom. Strader alone seems unable to make the step as he is assailed by doubt. He grieves that he will never again be able to find his way to the temple. But Theodora closes the scene with the prophecy that he will find his way to the light when his time has been fulfilled.

* * * * *

In the following dramas we see how the seeds of spiritual knowledge grow and develop in the various characters. Never can they remain at rest after any achievement. In each play fresh trials bring further progress in enlightenment. In the second, we follow the awakening of Capesius and witness the effect of memories of a previous incarnation on him, Johannes and Maria. The third and fourth are very much concerned with Strader, although the other characters also have to face their trials. It is noteworthy that each has to pursue an entirely different path to self-knowledge, but each needs the help and support of others. One of the leading themes is that of the redeeming quality of love and sacrifice. And as the members of the group come to spiritual awareness, so the reader finds a deeper understanding of the wisdom of Rudolf Steiner's representations of the sources of life.

THE SOUL'S PROBATION

Foreword

As explained in the introduction to the first Mystery Play, Rudolf Steiner, in these two dramas, was developing what had already come to expression in earlier forms. In the first, he was following the theme of Goethe's tale, *The Green Snake and the Beautiful Lily*. In the second, he was drawing upon a medieval legend with historical connections. It is told how the Knights Templar had occupied Burg Lockenhaus in the Austrian Burgenland, and there events had taken place, similar to those represented in the scenes from six to nine of *The Soul's Probation*.

In each of the four Mystery Plays, certain characters pass through trials which lead to enlightenment. We have seen in *The Portal of Initiation*, how Johannes, through an awakening in self-knowledge, received a vision of the future in which the many personalities, who had played a part in his development, were to be united in an occult brotherhood.

Now in the second drama, Maria, Johannes and Capesius, are to be brought to an experience of their life together in the Middle Ages and through this they learn to realise the debts they have incurred through this previous incarnation.

Scene One

THE LIBRARY AND STUDY OF CAPESIUS in a prevailing colour of brown. An evening mood.

When we first met Capesius at the beginning of

The Portal of Initiation, he was a doubter. As a historian, he had been especially interested in the ideas which had inspired the different cultural epochs, but, owing to his intellectual environment, he had come to the conclusion that thoughts are only shadow reflections of reality, while deeds have the power to shape events. Yet, after hearing Benedictus's lecture, he was stirred by the thought that words could work into the realm of will. His second enlightenment was brought about by the change in Johannes, from the despairing young artist to the confident friend who had asked to study history with him and had later painted his portrait. He had come to realise that this painting expressed qualities in his character which could not have been perceived by the physical senses. This experience led him to study the writings of Benedictus.

Some years have passed since the events depicted in the first scenes of *The Portal of Initiation*. In the first scene of *The Soul's Probation* we see Capesius pondering over words of Benedictus, but the ideas that are presented are so alien to his whole way of thinking that he is plunged into despair. As a typical representative of our modern age he has always considered that he himself has created his own thoughts. But now he realises that he has spun only illusory concepts about life and nature, which have always led him to doubt. He recognises that Johannes has come to attain an understanding of the spirit which can awaken powerful soul forces. He himself now feels that it is a sin to neglect such a quest. But he does not know how to develop these powers. His own way of thinking appears to him to be valueless; he has nothing on which to stand. He reads the words of Benedictus:

'Enter calmly into depths of soul
and let strong courage be your guide.
Cast off your former ways of thought
when you descend into yourself
to guide yourself towards selfhood.
As you extinguish self-engendered light,
the spirit's brightness will appear to you.'

Far from bringing light to Capesius, these words throw him into the deepest darkness. Benedictus' teaching has directed him not to soar with his abstract intellect into far distances but to realise that divine powers are at work within his own thinking, feeling and willing. This Capesius cannot yet experience.

In early days the leaders of humanity were well aware of their relationship with spiritual beings. But it became important for man to develop his individual powers, and then with his own energy to reunite with the divine world. The history of the Greeks illustrates this development. The guidance of priest-kings was no longer effectual. Spiritual knowledge was confined to the initiates of the Mystery Centres, and although their influence rayed out into many human affairs, leaders had to act out of their own intelligence. However at the same time a teaching was given by philosophers such as Socrates, Plato and Aristotle, so that, through the training of their thinking, human beings could once more find the spiritual worlds which had withdrawn. The knowledge of the divine origin of our thinking, feeling and willing has increasingly been lost and has led to the materialistic outlook of the present day. The experience that intellectual thinking leads only to a dead end can come as a great shock.

Capesius at this moment stands before the abyss. In the hour of his despair he has a supersensible experience. His soul forces appear before him. Luna, the inspirer of the will, summons him to put forth his strength. He must develop the courage to have hope and pour it into his will. Astrid, awakener of his thought life, calls to him to unite himself with the sun and stars so that the warmth of knowledge can fire him. But in our feelings it is more difficult for us to overcome the desire to give way to what pleases us, and Capesius has not freed himself from this weakness. Consequently, instead of meeting with the True Philia, he perceives the Other Philia.

Retardus makes his last appearance in the first play and the Other Philia now takes his place. Both hinder the human being from making an approach to the spirit world. The Other Philia appeals to Capesius' egoistic impulses and warns him not to listen to the guidance of Astrid and Luna, as she claims that they will lead him into vain delusions.

Capesius realises that Beings have spoken, but this leads him to doubt his own identity. Then his Spiritual Conscience speaks to him to assure him that his thoughts are now entering into the depths of human life, and his soul and spirit are soaring into cosmic realms from which he can receive renewing forces.

At this moment Benedictus enters. Capesius is grateful for his approach, as this alone has roused him from the horror of his state of confusion. Benedictus speaks of the link that binds them, but tells him that he will need to change his sense of values. His present misery is in reality good fortune, for one can lose only what severs one from cosmic being and, if one seems to lose what is of value, it can be found again and dedicated to a true aim. He does not offer any comfortable solution, but gives the confirmation that his words awaken spiritual power in those who are receptive. He warns Capesius that he is now ordained by destiny to a period of probation.

This scene illustrates the responsibility taken by a spiritual leader for those who have chosen to become his pupils. But at the same time the modern leader leaves his pupils free to accept or reject the guidance given. There is no question of dictating a way of progress.

Scene Two
A MEDITATION ROOM
We learn here that Maria and Johannes are also called upon to face a period of probation. Maria has again sought for Benedictus' guidance. Her natural healthy judgment has prompted her to feel that she must renounce her guidance of Johannes if he is to find his true goal. But she cannot accept this as a right impulse, since they have both been made aware of their lofty spiritual relationship.

Benedictus warns her that grief is misleading her. Her love is noble but love must also be guided by wisdom. Though she and Johannes have a long-standing connection which has guided him well, it is also important now that he should follow his own aims in freedom. Destiny does not require them to break their outer friendship, but it does demand his spiritual independence.

At first Maria finds this difficult to accept, since spirit powers have consecrated their eternal union. Benedictus points out that the web of destiny is complex and that she is seeing only one part of the truth. She has seen in imagination what the future holds, but her powers of will must transform it to reality. She needs to consider whether she has seen all her connections with Johannes in past lives.

Maria now shows how ready she is to accept her own shortcomings, and with what force of will she can undertake what is personally so painful. She makes her vow to Benedictus to transform her arrogance and leave her friend to develop his genius independently. Benedictus reassures her that if she can recognise what she has most valued in her love for Johannes she will find the strength to fulfil her duty.

Maria realises that part of her relationship with Johannes has been inspired by self-love. She calls on her three soul powers to give her the strength to change old ways of life and enter new spheres of will. Philia promises to imbue her with light of soul. Astrid will free her from fetters of desire, and Luna will call forth the strength to renounce, so that she may find traces of her past life in time's wide span. Maria is convinced that with their help she can free herself from the egoism which has blinded her. She realises that they can bring to maturity within her forces bestowed by the spiritual world.

The Spirit Voice of Conscience confirms that she is seeking to find what she owes in debt from a past life.

We see here that the Soul Forces, Philia, Astrid and Luna, are able to give fuller powers to Maria than to Capesius, as all depends on the ability of the recipient to receive their gifts. Capesius is unable to contact the true Philia. It is interesting also to compare how the Voice of Conscience speaks to Capesius of the source of thinking, arising from cosmic grounds, whereas with Maria the words refer to the guidance of life through the acceptance of duties owing to a debt from past lives.

Scene Three
A ROOM IN ROSE-RED with a cheerful atmosphere. Johannes at his easel.

Johannes has noticed that Maria made no comment when she last saw his painting, whereas hitherto she had always given him helpful guidance. He describes with joy how she has inspired him with courage to paint what the soul can experience in the spiritual world, how thought forms can transform matter, and colour bring the warmth of life. Without her help he would give way to discouragement. It seems so impossible to express in earthly guise what he can experience in the spirit. Yet when he yields himself to the spirit he realises that there is a spiritual art just as there is a spiritual science. However, when he is in doubt, he feels the need of Maria's inspiration.

At this moment Maria enters. She expresses pleasure that he has been so absorbed in his work that he has not noticed her; but he protests that he cannot create one picture without her guidance for it is her power which pours into him. His love for her saves him from falling into delusions.

Maria replies that if he were to paint out of his own inspiration there would be more unity in his work. Johannes cannot accept this; he is aware only that he would lose himself. He can express true spiritual experiences only by following her, for she can guide him to understand the living power of colour. On his own he is conscious of the instability of his feeling life. Maria points out that love which unites human beings should not destroy their individuality.

Left alone, Johannes is deeply disturbed. And now, like Capesius and Maria, he becomes conscious of the Soul Beings. Luna warns him that he cannot find his true identity mirrored in another soul. If he would truly express beauty in earthly form, he must have the courage to offer himself to spirit powers. Astrid appeals to him to transcend earthly love so that cosmic love may ripen within his heart. Like Capesius, Johannes is unable to contact the true Philia. The Other Philia tempts him not to listen to the summons which will lead him away from the earth into the freezing cold of cosmic heights.

In these three opening scenes we see how Capesius, Maria and Johannes are all called upon to face a coming trial. Maria shows herself well prepared as she has the strength to renounce personal feeling; but Capesius and Johannes are still in certain respects unripe.

Scene Four
THE LIBRARY AND STUDY OF CAPESIUS
We learn that it is a long time since Strader has visited Capesius. In reply to the latter's hearty welcome, Strader explains that he has had little leisure as his way of life has changed completely. He is now no longer struggling to solve life's problems in fruitless speculation, but is devoting himself to honest work which will be of some use to mankind. We gather that in the meantime he has had no connection with the circle around Benedictus.

When Capesius asks what are his aims, he says that it is useless to speak of understandable goals, for life is a treadmill which, when our strength is spent, throws us into darkness. Capesius is astonished that Strader, who used so courageously to try to solve the riddle of existence, can now renounce the quest. He assumes that it is from disappointed hopes. However, Strader refers to the seeress Theodora who made him recognise that his type of thinking could never find the sources of life. What he cannot understand is how such a revelation which seemed mere madness could awaken creative forces, for he recalls the young artist, who underwent such a change.

Capesius enquires whether the old problems do not haunt him from time to time. Strader acknowledges this but he feels that, as destiny has allowed no hope to enter his wasted life, renunciation may give him the strength to develop further in another existence, for he has come to the conclusion that the repetition of earthly life cannot be denied.

Capesius wishes that he could have come to such a conclusion as it would have brought him great relief. But Strader finds this truth cruel. It makes our experiences in life nothing but the consequences of what we really are. He reminds Capesius of how his parents had planned for him to enter the church and how his refusal had caused them great pain. Later he discovered that he was not really their child, so that he was a stranger in the world even before he was conscious. This confirmed in him the belief that he must have willed such a destiny, but he cannot perceive the powers that wove it for him. Now he regards the weaving of destiny as a kind of mechanical process and he has no interest in trying to discover how it works. Capesius feels convinced that Strader cannot long remain satisfied with this barren outlook.

It is apparent in this scene that Strader, like Capesius, is facing the abyss, but he has to travel a very different road. However the seed has been sown. It is remarkable how out of his own earnest struggle he has become convinced of the necessity of reincarnation. We have to remember the words of Theodora at the end of the first Mystery Play, that he too will find his way to the light when his time has been fulfilled.

Scene Five

THE LANDSCAPE AROUND THE BALDES' COTTAGE

Capesius once again seeks the solace of Felicia's fairy tales. She sees that he is weary and sorrowful but welcomes him gladly, although she and her husband no longer enjoy the peaceful solitude of former days. Many people are now seeking them out to gain something from Felix's knowledge. However, although formerly he wished only to develop his gifts in solitude, he now feels it is his duty to talk to those who come. Felicia regrets the old tranquil way of life.

Felix now appears and he too has changed during the last years. As a visionary, he had hitherto followed the custom of the early Rosicrucians, when spiritual wisdom was cultivated in secret; but he now realises that times have changed and knowledge of the spirit should be freely imparted to those who are open to receive it. We can here compare his approach to that of Rudolf Steiner who presented the discoveries of his research to all who sought for them. Felix states that they are now at a turning point of time and he is obeying the spirit guidance speaking within his own heart. He does not appear to acknowledge any influence from Benedictus, although we may well consider that his presence at Benedictus' lecture in the first scene of *The Portal of Initiation* showed interest in one who spoke out of a similar wisdom.

Felix knows that his way of speaking is little understood, for today it is expected that everything should be expressed in logical form, and so many regard him as a mere visionary, though others find it worthwhile to try to understand something of his meaning. He speaks a language which is imbued with spiritual life and so, though many do not grasp what he is trying to express, a seed has been sown which will gradually work on within them. Even if some have come out of unworthy motives, they have nevertheless heard truths which will later have their effect.

Felix assures Capesius that, as he is striving nobly, a time of enlightenment will come to him. He then describes the threefold nature of man. His head is a picture of the heavens; in his limbs spirits of the spheres are at work; within his breast beings of the earth are active. But a conflict takes place within man as moon demons try to interfere. Divine Beings have planned to bring together the forces of all the worlds, united in the form expressed in the body, soul and spirit of man.

Capesius cannot follow Felix's line of thought and is alarmed at the idea that man is the creation of Divine Beings. Felix adds a warning that the one who would know himself must beware of arrogance or he cannot attain spiritual wisdom.

Capesius now turns to Felicia for help and she weaves the teaching of Felix into a wonderful tale. It would be a travesty to retell her story and we will concentrate on only a few aspects.

The boy who grew up in the solitude of the forest was protected from all the achievements of modern civilisation. Hence he was able to perceive the hidden life of Nature and become at one with her. All aspects spoke to him of a spirit world. Where a spring gushed out of the rocks he was especially enchanted with the interplay of movement and light. Thus he was able to experience imaginatively the Beings who live in man's thinking, feeling and will, who appear to Maria as Philia, Astrid and Luna. In his vision, the first gathers the sparkling drops, the second forms a silvery chalice, and the third fills it with moonlight. But in the night he dreams that a fierce dragon robs him of his treasure. Four times he has the vision of the Beings of the spring, but then they appear no more; yet they live within his memory.

When twenty-one years later he is tired out with his work in the town and ponders about the direction of his life, suddenly the memory of his childhood vision rises before him. He beholds again the Beings of the well and they speak to his understanding soul. The experience has passed beyond the realm of imagination to that of inspiration.

The first, representative of Astrid, promises him that she can bestow on him the draught of hope; the second, corresponding to Philia, can give the courage of faith; and the third, Luna, offers the weaving of thought, that through bringing an understanding of life's problems and facing the void, develops the living rays of love.

That night he dreams again of the prowling dragon, but this time it cannot harm him for he is protected by the three Beings.

Capesius leaves Felicia feeling that blessing and health-giving forces have poured into him and, although the story was so simple, it has lifted his thoughts into unknown worlds. He wanders into the wood.

As Capesius departs, Johannes appears. He has been deeply troubled by Maria's firm decision that they should separate and is unwilling to accept it. His words show clearly that he is more dependent on her physical presence than on her spiritual leadership. This unrecognised sensual element leads him to a rude awakening. He now meets with a reflection of his lower unworthy self. Rudolf Steiner speaks of this as the Double.

As man becomes clairvoyant he is able to recognise his own being in the spiritual world; but when he lives in illusions, Lucifer and Ahriman are able to draw near. Ahriman then has the power to step beyond his rightful position in the physical world and give form and shape in the elemental world to what should remain an inner experience.

An awareness of this has been illustrated in literature during the last hundred years or so, for instance in Stevenson's *Dr. Jekyll and Mr. Hyde*. A very remarkable book appeared soon after the first world war. In *The Man who Found Himself*, Osbert Sitwell describes a young and penniless artist who meets with himself as he will appear when he is an elderly man who has deserted his principles in order to win success. He is filled with hate and indignation. Then in later years, bored and disillusioned, he confronts his own being as a young man. The shock causes his death.

Johannes hears his Double give expression to the sensual love that in reality he experiences for Maria; and he is shattered.

Now Lucifer and Ahriman appear to him. Here it is interesting to note that Lucifer appeals to Johannes to conquer himself and redeem him. He has already defeated Lucifer in the realm of imagination but not in his subconscious life.

Ahriman, on the other hand, urges Johannes to take courage to experience him fully, otherwise his life will remain barren.

During this incident Capesius has returned and becomes aware of all that Johannes has endured. He too is deeply shaken.

This experience has prepared both Johannes and Capesius for a vision into their past life together in the Middle Ages.

Scene Six
In the next four scenes we are transported into the early fourteenth century, and witness a series of scenes from the past lives of many of the characters who appear in the Mystery Plays. We watch those events which have brought about their problems and their relationships in their present lives.

We see a Templar Castle at the time when their Order is doomed to be destroyed. In 1119, Hugues de Payan and Geoffroi de Saint Adhémar had founded this Order of priest-knights to protect pilgrims on their way to Jerusalem. They were granted part of the palace built on the site of Solomon's Temple from which they derived their name. The movement grew rapidly and there were soon centres in all the Christian countries of Europe. By a special Papal Bull they were freed from any church authority except that of the Pope himself. An interesting feature of their Order was their admitting characters who had been excommunicated. These were allowed to change their names and begin a new life. The Pope approved of this as he realised the danger of undisciplined outlaws roaming the East beyond any control. The Templars organised the beginnings of a banking system. Crusaders could deposit money in one of their centres in Europe and draw out what they needed in the East. In this way the Templars became the possessors of very large sums of money, though none was available to individuals for all had taken on the vows of poverty, chastity and obedience.

Philip the Fourth of France became aware of their great wealth and was determined to possess it. As, through their connection with the East, the Templars had adopted a purer form of Christianity than that taught by the Catholic Church, he accused them of heresy and evil practices and was able to bring the Grand Master, Jacques de Molay, and a number of his followers to the stake. Philip forced the Pope to dissolve the Order in 1312 and the Grand Master met his death in 1314.

In the opening scene depicting the Middle Ages we first meet with twelve peasants. We need to realise that Rudolf Steiner pointed out that in the realm of our rational, calculable thinking there can be only twelve points of view. In imaginative thinking of course we are not limited to points of view.

These six men and six women are expressing their opinions about the Templar Knights and a Jew who is living in their neighbourhood. This character, who is making a study of nature and through his researches developing the art of healing, is none other than a previous incarnation of Strader. The views of the peasants range from racial antipathy to suspicion of his knowledge and his art of healing, jealousy of the favour shown him by the Knights of the Castle and even belief that he is working with evil powers. There are also doubts about the Knights. They are suspected of not being true to the Church, and of using the ignorant to do their devil's work. Seven of the peasants are negative because they are caught up in their traditions and cannot understand new impulses. But five express positive views. The hostile group foretell with pleasure the prospect of the Knights' overthrow; but those in sympathy realise that they are working to bring about a new order and are Christians although of a different outlook from that of the Church.

As the peasants leave the scene, Simon the Jew enters.

He expresses his feelings of pain at the senseless hate and scorn he meets on every side. But he believes that there is meaning in all that he and his race have to endure.

He sees himself in a similar position to the Knights, only they have chosen their isolation. He is grateful for permission to work on their land where he is able to study the secrets of the plants and minerals, for he is sure that in developing a knowledge of the sense world and the gifts of healing he is preparing a new knowledge for the future.

We see here how Simon is laying the foundation for his life as Strader, when his interest is to be directed towards the sense world and where, because of his present acceptance of a meaning in life, he is able to find his way to a knowledge of reincarnation.

We next meet with the master miner Thomas, who is none other than Johannes in a previous life. He is deeply disturbed, and when the Monk approaches, whom we know already as Maria, he confides his trouble. On the one hand he has experienced great joy, for he and the Overseer's daughter have confessed their love for each other; but on the other hand he has found that his father, whom he has long been seeking, is his superior, the First Preceptor of the Templar Knights, whom Thomas hates. The Monk, as a faithful follower of the Church, also is opposed to the Knights. He does not wish to separate father and son, but he relies on Thomas's devotion to his own teaching.

Scene Seven
This takes place in the Castle. The Grand Master is preparing his followers for their coming downfall. He speaks first of their high calling which is to bring aims inspired by the spiritual world into earthly life. He refers to their great leader, Jacques de Molay, who was condemned and put to death, though he does not mention him by name. Their enemies have become too strong for them to continue

their work on earth. Their Castle will be destroyed, but all they have done will bear fruit in the future. Those who have worked for them will suffer, but the seeds which have been sown within their souls will mature in a later earthly life. He asks his followers to stand loyally by him.

His words are not entirely understood. The First Master of Ceremonies, who is a former incarnation of Theodosius, and already shows that he lives predominantly in his feelings, is prepared to accept that the Order will be destroyed; but he cannot feel that it is right for the ignorant souls who work for them to be involved. The Grand Master shows that the life of individuals is also linked with the cosmic order. Those who are innocent will acquire new strength for a future life, while those who are guilty will atone for their wrongdoing. The First Master of Ceremonies cannot understand why the Templars should accept help from those who are evil, and is told that in striving for spiritual ideals one should work only with the good in imperfect souls, as in the process the evil will gradually be transformed.

The First Preceptor, who is none other than Capesius, is troubled that the enemy is stealing away many souls who have served the Knights, but he is assured that what has been laid in their hearts in this life will develop when they return to earth. As for the Knights themselves, it is incumbent on them to sacrifice their separate lives in the service of their high spiritual aims.

The words of the Grand Master reveal that the Templars had a different conception of Christianity from that of the Catholic Church. They were Manicheans in their understanding of good and evil. Manes, a Christian teacher who lived in Persia in the third century AD, held that evil should be overcome not by punishment but by working with whatever good lived within the heart of the evildoer. The knowledge of reincarnation also came from the East and had been lost in the West except in certain circles such as the Cathars and the Rosicrucians.

After the Grand Master's departure we hear other comments on his words. The First Preceptor complains that he is oppressed by the Grand Master's way of speaking about the spirit world as though it were physically present. The Second Master of Ceremonies, Romanus, already shows the certainty of his opinions and his strong will. He assures the First Preceptor that anyone who cannot accept the reality of the spirit worlds must be suffering from a hidden stain. This is true, for the First Preceptor, Thomas's father, deserted his wife and children to be free to follow a new way of life with the Templars.

As these two leave, the Monk enters. He has come to claim back a piece of land that had been lying idle until the Templars bought it some time previously for a small sum. They have since sunk a mine which has turned out to be a prosperous venture. The Monk claims that old deeds prove that the land legally belongs to the Church and should be restored. The Second Preceptor, Germanus, who receives him, replies in a spirited way that owing to the work given to many people and the substances mined which have served human needs, the land is theirs in the light of a higher justice. When the Monk implies that the Church will take action, the Preceptor declares that in that case the matter will be settled on the battlefield. It is doubtful if this is in tune with the teachings of the Grand Master. As they have reached an impasse, the Monk asks to see the Head of the Order.

While he is left alone, the Monk laments that he has to enter the residence of this hateful movement where he has to behold all kinds of devilish signs and images. At this moment he feels the approach of some supersensible power. A horror seizes him, but to his surprise he realises it is the Spirit of his former leader, Benedictus, the Head of the Dominican Order, who is no longer on earth. Benedictus summons the Monk to attend to him if he would awaken the clarity of thought necessary to bring spirit enlightenment. He describes how his followers, in clinging dogmatically to his teaching, misconstrue it. As times change, thoughts have to develop. Rightly interpreted, his words would indicate support of the Templar Knights, who are inspired from the spirit world with lofty aims for the future of mankind. The Monk is utterly bewildered. He cannot understand how these words can so conflict with all that the Dominicans are now teaching.

While he is standing in doubt, Ahriman and Lucifer appear to him. Ahriman points out that the Spirit of Benedictus now dwells in spirit heights and so cannot give the right guidance for earthly conduct. Lucifer, on the other hand, claims that the Templars are using the name of Christ to mislead the ignorant, while the real teaching is false.

The Monk decides that, if he remains faithful to his former leader, he will receive guidance. Benedictus is now able to appear to him again. He counsels him to meditate on the words Benedictus spoke on earth, until he is able to follow their thoughts into the spirit world and understand how they have become transformed.

Scene Eight
THE ROOM IN THE CASTLE
The Overseer, Joseph Kean, who is a former incarnation of Felix Balde, has sought an interview with the First

Preceptor. He begins with an assurance of his devotion to the Templar Order, but then expresses his deep concern that his daughter Celia and the Master Miner Thomas have declared their love and determination to marry. Celia is deeply religious and a follower of the Monk. As long as she was living at home, Kean had trusted that he would be able to awaken her understanding for the ideals of the Templar Order, but now that hope is lost. Thomas will win her over to his implacable hatred of the Knights.

The First Preceptor is obviously disturbed; but he replies that they have so many enemies that one more will hardly make any difference, and he can not interfere with the young people.

Kean now comes to the real meaning of his visit. Celia is not truly his daughter. He and his wife took her into their home when her father had deserted his family and her mother had died of grief. Kean has recently received papers which prove beyond doubt that the First Preceptor is her true father. In reality the Preceptor has known this for some time, but he did not expect that anyone else would come to know of his secret. He tells Kean that it is not possible for him to solve this problem at a moment's notice but that he should return again the next day.

Left alone, the First Preceptor realises that his wrongdoing has caught up with him. He left his wife and children because he felt they fettered him and he thought he could achieve a more rewarding life with the Templars. He has learned that this was egoism. Now that he hears the other Knights welcoming the prospect of death, because thereby they will be sowing seeds for man's future development, he knows that he is not worthy of this sacrifice. When he discovered his son Thomas he felt that heaven had forgiven him, and he decided to withdraw from the Templar Order and devote the rest of his life to his children. Now he realises he has lost them. He knows, however, what he must do. He must tell the young people the truth about their relationship. Then he must confide in the Grand Master and bear whatever penance is demanded of him.

When the First Preceptor has retired the Grand Master and Simon enter. The Grand Master is warning Simon that he must no longer leave the Castle as the false rumour that he deals in sorcery has roused too great a hostility. In reply to Simon's failure to understand why there should be hatred for those who wish to help them, the Grand Master explains that outer hatred and hostility are only the expression of the fight between good and evil which takes place in the individual human soul. We can compare this with the conclusion reached by Solzhenitsyn, after his ordeal in the labour camp and the prison hospital. We cannot overcome evil by fighting the evildoers. In that way we are ourselves drawn into evil. We can overcome it only in our own being, then we achieve the moral power to overawe or transform the wrongdoers.

Simon then confides an experience that he often meets with while wandering through the woods and fields in search of healing herbs. He is approached by a figure who stretches out his hand with an expression of the most wonderful love and compassion. Simon longs to fall at his feet in worship; but then without his conscious control, he is seized with the most violent feelings of hate and rage. He is also very much drawn to the teaching of the Templar Knights, but then doubts assail him. He fears that in all his lives to come his ideals will be undermined by this involuntary opposition and doubt. Far from being in any way shocked, the Grand Master is moved by Simon's vivid description and it brings to him a vision of how spirit powers link world goals with human destiny.

As the Grand Master and Simon leave, the two Masters of Ceremonies come into the room. The First Master (Theodosius) is still troubled by the leniency of their Grand Master, but the Second (Romanus) now gives a masterly summary of the essential teaching of the Templar Knights. Their aim is to understand all human souls; hence they cannot oppose those who are not yet mature enough to follow their deeper meaning. The Knights know that through spirit vision men in the future will be able to behold the Being of the Sun who came once to earth. But the Leader of their Order taught them that they must allow souls gradually to mature before they can understand the deeper truths. And even when they have passed the first test and know the truth of reincarnation, they have to face a second trial and overcome the danger of pride which will lead them into delusions. The Knights must give up the idea that they can easily pass on the spirit wisdom that they have themselves attained. Many today who oppose them have received unconsciously a seed which will develop and bear fruit in later lives. The First Master is prepared to accept these words of highest wisdom but finds it difficult to follow them in this present life. To this the Second replies that he can accept their Leader's words that it is not possible for all men to live the future in advance, but it is important that some can foresee the future and dedicate their lives to liberate new forces and guard them for eternity.

Scene Nine
Joseph Kean, his wife and their daughter Bertha are in the woodland green that we saw in Scene Six.

Bertha is asking her mother to tell one of the stories that her father brings back from the Knights. She describes herself as a simple little thing who does not understand learned words. She goes to sleep when Thomas speaks about his science. As Bertha is the previous incarnation of the Other Maria, we see that she carries her feeling qualities into her next life. Thinking is alien to her but she absorbs truths through the stories which Joseph Kean assures her carry spiritual truths beyond death. Dame Kean, who is none other than Felicia, has already the gift for telling stories. The tale which she now tells illustrates the Templar Knights' teaching of good and evil. These are not separate inimical principles as taught by the Catholic Church, but spring from the same source. They have grown apart in the course of time. The handle of the axe which cuts down the trees was shaped from the wood of the oak. The implication is that one day they will be reunited.

Rudolf Steiner has shown that, whereas the problem for the fourth civilisation, dominated by the Greeks and Romans, was that of death, the problem for our age is that of evil. The Templar Order was preparing an understanding for how man's thinking had to lose its connection with the spirit world in order that we could achieve self-consciousness. The loss of divine guidance led man to fall into error so that out of his own effort he might find the way to reunite himself with the spirit.

As the Keans take their departure, the twelve peasants approach. Those who are hostile to the Knights and the Jew are delighting in the news that opponents are closing in upon the Castle. They are eager to join in the attack and one boasts that he will lead the way by a secret passage of which he had learned while working for the Knights. Those with a kind of atavistic clairvoyance are pleased to relate visions of the seizing of the Castle through the guidance of a traitor. But the wiser group warns of the horrors of war and the Sixth Woman remains loyal to her belief that only through Christ can they find the right way.

We learn something important from the Sixth Man. Though he is a devout follower of the Monk, he has not been able to understand his latest sermon. At his next appearance, this is made clear. As the peasants notice the Monk's approach, they retire so as not to disturb his meditations. We find that the Monk already displays the quality which characterises Maria. He is prepared to acknowledge his own failures. He realises that his meeting with Lucifer and Ahriman is a sign of his lack of inner harmony and that he must continue to meditate the teaching of his Master in order to acquire inner calm. He has been misled by vanity which the Templars recognise as the second trial to be faced on the path of spiritual development.

The scene ends with a meeting between Celia, who is a former incarnation of Theodora, and Thomas. They have been brought together through their blood relationship, and Thomas realises that his longing for his father was in reality his quest for Celia. Celia shows that even in this incarnation she has certain clairvoyant experiences which arise through love. She tells her brother that before she met him she had a vision in which his likeness appeared to her. He told her tenderly that, though she had been deserted as a child, she was still supported by love, and, if she could wait in patience, love would again find the way to her. Thomas has not Celia's capacity for affection. He complains that an impassable gulf must separate him from her adopted parents. Celia tries to persuade him that understanding is possible between them. The image of her brother had spoken words of comfort to her.

> 'Out of the Godhead rose the human soul;
> dying it can descend to depths of being;
> it will in time release from death the spirit.'

Later she learned that these words were a motto of the Knights.

But Thomas is adamant. He considers that he would be betraying what he believes to be the truth if he came to any understanding with those who support a false doctrine.

Celia is deeply grieved, especially at his rejection of their father, and she would not know how to bear the pain if it were not for her faith that in the end love always overcomes hate.

With this scene the episodes from the Middle Ages come to an end.

Scene Ten
THE WOODLAND SCENERY AND THE BALDES' COTTAGE IN THE BACKGROUND

The following events follow those in the first three scenes.

Only three of the characters have consciously experienced their lives in the fourteenth century. Maria, Johannes and Capesius, owing to their stern awakening, were prepared for this vision into their previous lives.

We first meet with Capesius who is slowly returning from his soul wanderings. He is in a state of confusion as he is still aware of himself in the life between death and a new birth. He is conscious of a painful and compelling urge to reincarnate, which oppresses him. But he realises that this springs from a previous condition of a complete lack of the sense of his own individuality. He was aware of being expanded into the whole cosmos. Out of the wide spaces he heard resounding the words:

'O Man, know thou thyself within thy world.'

Then a being, whom he recognised to be a reflection of his own soul, continued, 'Unless you feel this being interwoven with you, you are a dream that only dreams itself'.

Capesius strove to remember what preceded the period of chaos. A series of pictures of people and events pass before his eyes. He feels connected with their world but observes it without any emotion. He feels as though he were raising these scenes out of the deep well of memory and gradually comes to recognise the characters he knows in his present life in their medieval setting. Johannes was his son, the Master Miner Thomas, and the seeress Theodora was his daughter. He knows Maria as the Monk who opposed his Order and separated him from his son.

Again he finds himself blissfully borne into the far spaces of the spirit. Then gradually he wakes into the consciousness of his present life. He is in the woodland near the Baldes' cottage and his past experiences are weighing on him like an unbearably heavy load which changes into a nightmare of conflicting forces.

Then the Voice of Spirit Conscience speaks to him. He is summoned to make something of what he has seen and out of spirit light recreate his life.

Scene Eleven
A MEDITATION ROOM

Maria is confronted by Ahriman who is trying to persuade her that her vision of the past has been spun out of her own delusions. Benedictus has led her astray by presenting her with untruths so that she has created a series of pictures which are merely distortions of her own present experiences. He can prove this without the possibility of doubt because she has pictured the characters in the same sex and dispositions as they have in their present lives.

Maria is able to withstand Ahriman. She accuses him of being the father of deceit and yet she recognises that he sometimes tells the truth when it serves his purpose. Thus it is important for human beings to develop an awake consciousness and in this way they can develop a sound judgment. By recognising Ahriman's true position, Maria is able to answer him. She asks him whether he has the power to penetrate every period of the past. Ahriman replies that no spirit would refuse him entry to any sphere he wished to enter. To this Maria replies that though Ahriman has given man the power of thought, there is one realm he cannot enter, and that is when thought has been raised into spirit wisdom. She will now try to forge this sword of spirit truth in which case he will have to retire. She then describes how there are certain turning points of time when old forces have to die away so that new ones may emerge. At such times it is important for certain souls to bring powers from a previous life into their succeeding one. She and her friends were united in the spiritual world with a brotherhood which was preparing to sow seeds which would need a long while to mature. Hence men appeared as men, women as women. The period between the incarnations was also shorter than usual. She accuses Ahriman of lacking the insight to see into such times. She reminds him of how they met each other in the Templar Castle where he had tried to stimulate her self-conceit through flattery. The recollection of this event gives her the strength to withstand him.

Maria has understood Ahriman in his true being. On

the one hand, on drawing man down into the sense world, he has given him the power of accurate observation and freedom of thought. But Ahriman's intention is to keep man fettered to his sense experiences and cut him off from the spiritual world. In this way he is the father of deceit. Maria is grateful for the gift of independent thinking, but she shows Ahriman that when this is raised to sense-free spirit truth, he can no longer touch it. To the sound of thunder, Ahriman is driven away.

Scene Twelve
THE SAME ROOM AS IN SCENE ELEVEN
Lucifer appears to Johannes and points out to him how Capesius has attained insight into a previous life without acquiring the strength to face its challenges. He now knows his obligations for all coming lives, but achievement depends on will power which Capesius has not yet developed. His spiritual vision will only dazzle him, for he will not know how to fulfil all his tasks in one life.

Johannes now falls under Lucifer's spell. He feels that he has been led into spiritual heights for which he is entirely unfitted. He thought he was able to represent supersensible worlds in interweaving colours; but the image of himself which appeared to him as his Double has shown him the dreadful truth. He imagined he was inspired by the purest love, when in reality sensual passion was surging through his veins. Surely the soul that lived in the Miner Thomas is unworthy of following the spiritual path along which Johannes has been led in his present life. He has been striving to attain what will be possible only in future ages.

The cosmic will must know the goal of life, so he will submit to it and no longer try to suppress it by conscious spiritual striving. He accepts Lucifer's claim to be a part of the cosmic will which gives man freedom and feels that he must learn to know Lucifer, not only in the realm of ideas, but in his depths of will.

Scene Thirteen
THE TEMPLE OF THE HIDDEN MYSTERIES as in the last Scene of the first Mystery Play. A Spiritual Vision.
Enter Lucifer and Ahriman.

Lucifer has won the power to enter the Temple of the Sun owing to his victory over Johannes, but he complains that his success will be short-lived unless Ahriman also overcomes Maria. Ahriman replies that the times are not propitious to him. Another character is approaching on whom he has also been steadfastly at work, but though Strader is coming to the Temple in ignorance, his energy in grappling with his thinking power is leading him forward.

As Ahriman retires, Philia, Astrid and Luna approach with Strader. Philia undertakes to imbue herself with trust from the living forces of striving, so that the spirit sleeper may be awakened. Astrid promises to bring the rays of hope shining into the darkness, so that the sleeper may be upheld by joy. Luna will bring warmth with the force of love so that he may be freed from his cosmic burdens.

Benedictus, Theodosius and Romanus now enter. Benedictus calls on his companions to assist him in bringing spirit light to those who are seeking but cannot yet come to full vision. Supersensible powers are with them in this holy place. Philia with her gift of faith can transform the astral body of man. Astrid through awakening hope can open etheric forces to life-giving powers. And Luna in strengthening the will can arouse love for all mankind. In this way they open Strader's being to the Christ whom he rejected in his life as Simon. We see here how both human and spirit beings are at work to help those who strive towards the light. Benedictus shows that at times the soul of man is open to the light, but at others it sinks into darkness, and then the members of the Temple ray out their help. When Strader comes to realise that his abstract thoughts about Nature are only his own theories, he will seek for the reality in all around him.

Benedictus now speaks of another character who is seeking for the light but has not the strength to approach the Temple. Capesius in his pursuit of thinking has developed certain spiritual powers, but his recognition of errors in a past life made him doubt his powers ever to redeem these. Romanus states that with the aid of the Temple, Capesius will learn that men have to bear many burdens that cannot be solved in only one incarnation. When he is able to go boldly ahead and meet the Guardian, he will learn that one cannot fulfil one's destiny without pain; for pain strengthens the will to attain enlightenment.

Benedictus now informs Lucifer that his power to enter the Temple will be short-lived. Maria has performed deeds that will soon bear fruit. At his words Maria appears and Benedictus is able to describe how in a past life Johannes was faithful to her even when she opposed the light from the Templar Order which she now upholds. The firmness of such a bond is beyond Lucifer's power. Maria adds that there are springs of love which he can never touch, and that is when faults of former lives are taken up and transformed by a free act of sacrifice. She herself in that past life separated Johannes from his father. She now makes it her task to assist Capesius. Although Johannes, from time to time misled by desire, strays from the paths of light, she has confidence in his star and in her relationship with him.

Benedictus explains how in an earlier life the threads of destiny of three people had become entangled. But now within the Temple a lofty spirit light shines upon this knot. He calls upon Maria, who is now the only one of the three to be present in this holy place. He summons her to ray out her light so that those powers which worked destructively in earlier times may now become forces of healing. In their past lives the father could not win the love of his son; now he will be able to accompany him on their spirit paths. Benedictus entrusts Maria to maintain Johannes' soul within the light. We see that Maria has now won a position among the assistants of the Temple of the Sun. Benedictus tells her that as she has given Johannes his freedom, he will turn to her again when he has found his independence. If she remains loyal to the Temple, Johannes will long for her even in the realm where Lucifer holds sway. He will find his way to the light; for the one who has consciously beheld the spirit heights from the depths of his soul can pass through light and darkness without his powers being destroyed. He has breathed the air of eternity which raises him from the depths into the region of the Sun.

THE GUARDIAN OF THE THRESHOLD

Foreword
The last two plays of this series are introduced not by the phrase 'through Rudolf Steiner' but 'by' him. He was no longer relying on themes such as Goethe's tale or the legend of the Templar Centre, but was following the development of his characters through his own spiritual knowledge. Harry Collison in his *Commentaries* describes how just before the production of *The Guardian of the Threshold* Rudolf Steiner and his supporters had parted company with the theosophists, so that he was freer to develop what he had to give in a manner that any intelligent unprejudiced thinker who was seeking a path of spiritual knowledge would be able to follow. This situation is reflected in the first scene of the *Guardian of the Threshold* where a Rosicrucian Brotherhood has decided that their spiritual wisdom should no longer be kept secret but should be made available for all who are able to understand it. In our present time it is important for man to take some responsibility for his own progress so that in due course he will be able consciously to pass the Guardian of the Threshold.

In *Knowledge of the Higher Worlds* Rudolf Steiner has described two Guardians. The Lesser is the creation of our own being out of our many incarnations, expressing all our faults and failings. In general this is concealed from us until we have made considerable progress in spiritual knowledge. The soul who has been rightly prepared for this experience will realise now that he has gradually to transform and turn to good all that has been done amiss; but for the one who is insufficiently prepared, the meeting with this Being comes as a great shock.

The Greater Guardian is the lofty Spiritual Being who protects the higher worlds from those who are unworthy to enter.

In this play we see how the different characters approach the Guardian.

A considerable time has elapsed since the events described in the first Mystery Play. Hans Pusch has reckoned it at 13 years, whereas Collison suggests 15. We have the following guide: we are told that three years have passed between the events in the first and second sections of *The Portal of Initiation*. In *The Soul's Probation*, Capesius and Strader meet after a long separation, but no mention is here made of Strader's connection with Theodora. In *The Guardian of the Threshold*, Scene Four, we learn that they met in Capesius' house and became good friends. In this scene they are celebrating the anniversary of their marriage, which took place seven years earlier.

In the course of the Mystery Plays, we see how the characters do not necessarily improve from incarnation to incarnation. Though in one lifetime they may have achieved a high level, in the next they are presented with entirely new problems and for a while may seem to fall. However, gradually they struggle to redeem their failures.

Scene One
THE WAITING ROOM TO THE SANCTUARY OF THE ROSICRUCIAN BROTHERHOOD
In early performances four pictures, of Elijah, of John the Baptist, of Raphael and of Novalis, were shown to

illustrate the different manner of initiation according to the changes of time. The prevailing colour of the room is blue.

A number of people have been invited to meet with representatives of the Rosicrucian Brotherhood. Together with Strader and Felix Balde there are twelve who are reincarnations of the peasants who appeared in the medieval scenes of *The Soul's Probation*. At that time they had made uneasy connections on the one hand with the Templar Movement and on the other with Simon the Jew. In their present lives they are developing their relationships. However, changes have taken place in the period between death and a new birth and now they express themselves through their mental attitudes rather than their sympathies and antipathies. As a sign that they are more individualised they are here given separate names. We later learn from Scene Eight that they represent the twelve possible points of view and their responses to the Rosicrucian invitation vary from appreciation to suspicion of the Mystic League and doubt about the reasons for the invitation.

Ferdinand Reinecke, who takes the lead in the conversation, is contemptuous of all spiritual striving and has a high opinion of his own shrewd common sense, while Michael Edelmann considers that the Brothers are good and should be supported. Maria Treufels feels that Strader is better qualified to lead them than the Rosicrucian Brothers as only through him will come the good forces to lead to a better future. Strader thanks her for her words and finds it necessary to explain what he has been doing. He has long been troubled that, through the introduction of machinery, workers are driven more and more to live ugly and meaningless lives. At first he thought the real solution was for human beings to learn to be interested in one another, but he has lately found out that there must be a wholly different attitude to work. He is constructing a device which will enable workers to live in settings of their own choice and work in their own style without being forced into factories. So far this has been only theoretical but his device has been tested and specialists have found it seemingly workable.* Strader now sees the necessity of uniting with those who are wise in spiritual values.

Felix Balde describes his own approach to the spirit world. He came in solitude by the path of mysticism, but he can admire Strader's way of development through a higher knowledge of the sense world. He now sees how important it is that what he had followed in private should be open to all to discover, hence he supports the invitation of the Rosicrucian Brotherhood.

Three raps are heard, and the Grand Master, followed by three of his supporters, comes into the room.

We have met the first speaker as Romanus in *The Portal of Initiation* and as the second Master of Ceremonies in the Templar Order. He is now known as Frederick Trautman. He describes how their Grand Master has recognised from signs of the times that their sacred wisdom should no longer be held in secret, but should be presented in a form that any clear thinker seeking a path of spiritual knowledge will be able to follow. They have found a character who can fulfil this. Thomasius, who is known as Johannes when following

---

*In 'The Challenge of the Times', (6 lectures, Dornach, 29 November/8 December 1918) Rudolf Steiner says, '...solely by means of certain capacities that are still latent but evolving in man, and with the help of the law of harmonious oscillations, machines and mechanical constructions and other things can be set in motion. A small indication is to be found in what I connected with the person of Strader in my Mystery Dramas.' (Lecture 3, page 93, Anthroposophic Press, New York).

his artistic career, has shown that he can express their deepest spiritual truths in a language that can be understood by scientists, so the Mystic League is inviting him to unite with its work.

Magnus Bellicosus, known as Gairman in *The Portal of Initiation* and as the Second Preceptor in the Templar Order, gives a sketch of the progress of Johannes/Thomasius. He describes how as an artist Johannes was inspired by a spiritual teacher so that in colour and form he was able to express supersensible ideas which appeared as though magical; but recently when he could have risen still higher in his artistic career, he decided to turn to science so that he could express spirit wisdom in a form that many people would be able to follow and understand. This sacrifice has been of great assistance to many seekers of a path of higher development.

Hilary, the Grand Master, who was also the leader of the Templar Order, now describes the spiritual progress of mankind. There was a time in early years when human beings were still too undeveloped to be able to guide themselves and were led by angelic beings. These then chose certain suitable characters to be initiated and help in the progress of mankind. Gradually as these men became capable of choosing to learn from them, the spiritual beings withdrew and the chosen initiates through their own efforts contacted the higher worlds for guidance. It is a long process for human beings to become ripe enough to understand all that was taught in the Mysteries, but the time has come when many people now out of their own initiative are able to reach a level enabling them to assist their fellow men.

Ferdinand Reinecke objects that Hilary has made an unnecessarily elaborate description of this process.

Thomasius' book will stand or fall by its own merits. It does not need any connection with the Mystic League. To this Albertus Torquatus, known in *The Portal of Initiation* as Theodosius and as the First Master of Ceremonies in *The Soul's Probation*, replies that if one took Thomasius' book only for itself it would not fulfil its intention. Its full meaning is to lead the average reader to accept spiritual ideas so that he wishes to go further, and thus it makes a bridge to the teaching of the Rosicrucians. With these words the scene closes.

It is often puzzling to readers that the three characters who support Hilary appear so one-sided in the first scene of *The Portal of Initiation*. There Romanus' whole interest is given to the world of machinery; Germanus, as he is called in the original German version, is the mocker. But perhaps we can see them as representing the characteristics of different cultures which have given their influence to Europe. The Romans were gifted in dealing with the material world; hence their creation of aquaducts, roads, central heating systems and so on. The Germanic people were warlike as a tribe, hence Germanus's later name of Magnus Bellicosus; and this is shown in his character as the Second Preceptor in the Templar Order when he so readily opposes the Monk. The Anglo-Saxons are especially given to treating incidents with humour. However, Germanus though a mocker shows an openness to the teaching of Benedictus. Perhaps Hans Pusch has changed the name of Germanus to Gairman as he does not wish to associate him only with the German tribe of the Nordic people. It is the English who tend to meet what is over-serious with humour and this is difficult for many Germans to understand. He may also wish to bring the name more into connection with the first description of Germanus, as the prototype of the spirit of the earth brain, (Greek Ύεα). Theodosius, as the representative of feeling, can perhaps be connected with the Celtic world, for the cult of Arthur's round table was for the development of nobler feeling. His knights, by serving a cause worthier than themselves, elevated their own personal feelings. For example, for the honour of Arthur's court, Gawain was prepared to marry the Loathly Lady.

All three characters were drawn in earlier incarnations into the spiritual movement of the Templars, and in the light of this were able to find their way again into the Mystic League of the Rosicrucians, but in their private lives they still carry with them something of their tribal characteristics.

It is interesting that at this period of time women are admitted to an occult movement. At the time of the Templar Order and of the Rosicrucian Brotherhood there were no women members; but just as private individuals who have attained a certain level of spirit consciousness can be admitted, so too it is important that women should play their part.

Scene Two
THE SAME ANTECHAMBER AS IN SCENE ONE
The twelve representatives of the public have left. Hilary stands with his three supporters, together with Strader and Felix Balde, and Thomasius and Maria have been admitted.

Hilary starts with words of welcome to Thomasius. He considers that what Thomasius has achieved deserves the seal of both the wisdom of the Ancient Mysteries and the teaching of the Mystic League, and so he is invited to unite with them. Magnus Bellicosus assures Thomasius that he can now be reunited with his spiritual leader and with the friend who withdrew from him to give him his freedom. She is here to welcome him.

Thomasius now gives them all a great shock. He states that if he were the man they think him to be he would be honoured to accept their invitation, but he has received a clear flash of knowledge. On his way to this meeting he had encountered Ahriman. For several years he had served Lucifer and imagined that he knew Lucifer well, but all unknown to himself, strong desires were concealed deeply within him. These drove him under the spell of Ahriman and his work is really inspired by Ahriman. Although what he has achieved may be good, Ahriman will claim his reward and then Thomasius himself will be obliged to turn its results to evil. He could bear this for himself alone, but if he joins the League it will cause their destruction. He now blames the members of the Rosicrucian Brotherhood, as leaders of the spiritual life of the time, for not having recognised that his book was the work of Ahriman.

In reality it was a true insight into his own nature and his relationships with Lucifer and Ahriman. We can see from the fact that Strader, Felix Balde and Hilary all regarded his work as conveying important truths, that it was difficult at the turn of the century for thinkers to recognise the influence of Ahriman. Members of the Rosicrucian Brotherhood were still living under the guidance of a spiritual teaching which was no longer fitted to the times, and Strader and Felix Balde, having struggled in loneliness to find their own path, were unable to recognise fully where Ahriman held sway. These characters had not yet consciously passed the Guardian of the Threshold, which alone could have given them the assured power to distinguish between truth and error.

Hilary now realises, however, that they can no longer collaborate with Thomasius, but must wait for signs from the spiritual world.

All except Thomasius and Maria leave the stage.

* * * * *

In a circle of light the spiritual forms of Philia, Astrid and Luna appear, concealing Maria. They speak from their different natures to Thomasius of the longing of the soul and spirit for the light of the supersensible world and converse with gods, which can be attained through vision and courage. However, they are warning him that the soul whose thinking is bound to the sense world becomes lost and cannot reach the realms which divine beings wisely conceal from those who are not prepared.

Thomasius then becomes aware of the world conscience, warning him that what had upheld him until now is lost and he is wandering in the abyss where those must stray who seek for the divine world merely out of a longing for their own satisfaction. He shudders at the void and lacks the courage to be able to see the new growth that can come through facing the darkness without hope of consolation.

The spiritual voice of Maria is heard, although she herself is unseen. She calls on Thomasius to remember the warmth of hope and the light of creativity he had received in earlier years through love, and now in the loneliness of his darkest hour to remember that his companion is with him once more.

Thomasius realises he has been given a vision of his own soul's confusion but the voice of love has come as consolation. The light fades and the spirit beings disappear, leaving Maria and Thomasius facing each other. Maria assures him that she can now accompany him into the darkness of the ever empty fields of ice where men are called upon to create new life out of seeming death. He has come to a turning point in his life, where he has to make a new start, but he must never wish that what has happened should have been different. It weakens the soul to look back and regret and wish that things had been otherwise. Whether one walks ahead on the true path or wanders, one still can learn from all that happens and thus gain new strength. He must now wait in silence for the spirit's guidance, for he must find his own being anew. He has often come to the Threshold where the Guardian keeps watch, but has always turned aside. Now Maria will lead him past the Guardian. He will be able to go with her as his companion, and he must be prepared to face whatever happens to him when he crosses the Threshold.

We can see from this scene that Maria is already able to pass the Guardian. She is the only one so far, apart from Benedictus, who has attained this power.

Scene Three
LUCIFER'S DOMAIN
There are no enclosing walls, but many fantastic forms of plants, animals and other shapes surround the stage. Lucifer's vacant throne is to the left. The souls of Capesius and Maria are facing each other.

Maria is surprised that her first meeting in this realm is with the one she knew on earth as Capesius. He is unwilling to listen to his name or to hear about the earth, which he regards as a place where human beings have only shadow pictures of spiritual realities. Maria reproaches him for speaking like one who has never incarnated. Those who have lived on earth know that it is not insignificant, but that man can learn there secrets of the connection between the earth and the cosmos, and so gain strength. Capesius dreads living on earth again. To him it is a prison, where man loses contact with all the beauty he has known in the spiritual world. He himself does not understand the speech of ordinary human beings unless they describe the spirit and he fears any new earthly life and longs to be free of future incarnations.

Maria replies that he must surely recognise that even though man can form only shadow pictures on earth they are of great beauty and they sow the seeds of future ripening. Only through earthly life can man acquire strength in his true 'I'. Capesius hates the word 'I'; he says that in the realm of Lucifer it burns him. Maria is surprised, since no soul can find its way to Lucifer's domain that has not received the 'I', but Capesius tells her he has learned from Lucifer that those who come into his kingdom when their 'I' is still dreaming can do him no harm; it is only when man has developed ego forces that these burn here.

He now reminds Maria that she owes him a karmic debt; and in order to repay him, he asks her to arrange with Lucifer that she can protect him in future lives on earth.

Although it is not actually mentioned in their conversation, Capesius is really suffering from the effects of his insight into his incarnation in the Middle Ages, when he deserted his family in order to join the Templars. He has been filled with a great dislike for his own being as he experiences it. This is referred to when he claims that Maria owes him a debt. As the Monk, she brought about the separation between Thomas the Miner (Johannes) and his father the First Preceptor (the previous incarnation of Capesius).

Maria realises that she has learned a great deal from this meeting with the soul of Capesius, and she willingly accepts

THE GUARDIAN OF THE THRESHOLD 73

the debt, which she undertakes to repay.

Capesius now disappears and Lucifer comes forward. We hear from him that Maria has come to him to request self-knowledge for Johannes. Although she is now once more Johannes' guide, she realises that he is still prone to become a prey to violent changes of feeling and therefore liable to fall under Lucifer's sway.

Lucifer asks how she can request this favour from him when Benedictus whom she follows is his arch enemy. Johannes has for some time left the leadership of Benedictus and now Lucifer himself will become his guide and give him all that he requires of self-knowledge.

During Lucifer's speech, Benedictus appears. He tells Lucifer that he must now listen to Maria because her words have power as a result of former deeds. Maria has made a solemn holy vow within her heart that she will bring healing forces to Johannes, so that she may rescue him from his many temptations. If Lucifer would only for a while withdraw his own brilliant light of selfish quest for power, he would feel the strength of Maria's vow.

Maria now adds to her words. She knows that Johannes will have to be approached in quite a different way. Lucifer cannot have the right effect upon him by direct influence. He is planning to work upon Johannes' Double, who will appear before him. Lucifer feels the power of Maria's words.

(There enter from opposite sides, Johannes/Thomasius*

---

*The name Johannes is used when this character is being guided by Maria, and is under the influence of Lucifer. The Double is an Ahrimanic figure, and the name Thomasius is used when Johannes/Thomasius is under the influence of Ahriman. However, it is noticeable during this play that Lucifer and Ahriman sometimes play into one another's hands and hence it is Lucifer who calls up the Ahrimanic Double.

and his etheric Double).

Johannes/Thomasius addresses the Double* by saying that he has not seen him for a long time and that he used to be frightened of him, but now he can meet him calmly. He resents the Double's leaving him unfree and wishes to escape his influence. The Double replies that he has been constantly with Johannes/Thomasius in the hidden depths of his soul, but that during the last years when Thomasius was giving all his attention to clear thinking, the Double had become transformed and so in his own being is free from Thomasius' passion for Maria. He now claims the right from Lucifer to work himself upon Thomasius.

Lucifer feels that this aim is good but warns the Double that he cannot do as he wishes or the result would be a complete coldness and lack of feeling. He himself must now take on the further development and imbue Thomasius with a love as powerful as that which he once felt for Maria.

Benedictus realises that the noble work that he and Maria are striving to do for Johannes will be ruined if Lucifer has his way and Johannes will turn to evil the scientific teaching which he has given to the world. On the other hand, if his friends can support him, this clear thinking can be turned to good for the benefit of mankind.

Maria is afraid that Johannes will be lost to them and Benedictus affirms that this will be so if everything con-

---

*For further information about the 'Double', see 'The Wrong and Right Uses of Esoteric Knowledge', lectures given in Dornach, 18th–25th November 1917, especially the first lecture. Also 'The Secrets of the Threshold', lectures given in Munich, 24th–31st August 1913, see lecture 7. Both books published by Rudolf Steiner Press, London.

tinues as it is at present developing, but if she herself can summon her earnest vow with sufficient strength she will be able to stand against the forces of Lucifer. Lucifer realises that he is receiving strong opposition and so calls up all his powers. He summons the soul of Theodora. She is unhappy to find herself in this strange place as her spiritual visions have always brought her joy and calm. Now the Double is seized with tremendous longing for her, which will stream out as an influence on Johannes.

Benedictus appeals to Maria, as the crucial moment has come. She must now call forth the full power of her vow. Maria challenges Lucifer. She states that first he brought into the world wisdom before the time was ripe. Man should have developed more slowly in the care of the gods, but now Lucifer is using another weapon. When Johannes has developed clear thinking to free himself from Lucifer, the latter is attacking him by awakening sensual love. However, she will combat this danger, for she has made a solemn earnest vow that in order to bring healing forces to Johannes she herself will forego all joy in the achievement of spiritual thoughts; and then when Johannes is apt to say that only through love can he become a true being she will give him the answer that the fruits of love can be attained by man only when they spring from the realm of the gods.

Lucifer proudly declares that he means to fight, but Benedictus replies that in fighting, Lucifer will serve the gods.

It is a problem to many readers that Lucifer should be able to exert power over so pure a being as Theodora. Harry Collison, in his commentaries, throws some light on this theme. Owing to the purity of her astral body and ego, which are fully aware of the spiritual world, he cannot draw Theodora into evil; but she has never developed her sense-free thinking, for her visions have come to her by nature. In the Temple of the Sun in the first play she is represented with wings, which show her as one who is free from earthly bonds. Because of her lack of sufficient interest in the life of the senses, Lucifer has access to her etheric powers. This throws her into a kind of confusion which will become apparent in the next two scenes.

Scene Four
A ROOM IN STRADER'S HOUSE predominantly rose red in colour. Strader and his wife Theodora are sitting at their separate work tables. It is the anniversary of their wedding seven years ago. Strader is led to remember the events by which he and Theodora were drawn together.

He had seen her first at the meeting of Benedictus' group, when she had given her revelation of the future appearance of Christ in the Etheric World. Later he had observed the change in Johannes due to the influence of his spirit training; but he had never been able to understand any of Benedictus' teaching. The only effect of his connection with this group was his loss of faith in reason and strict scientific thought. As he could then find no answer to his problems about the meaning of life he was thrown into darkness and he sought relief in absorbing all his forces in technical work. Then he met Theodora and they became good friends.

Theodora finds it natural that he should like to go over these old memories. She recalls how she herself used to visit the Baldes in their mountain solitude, as Felix gave her good guidance and with his help her spiritual powers matured. There she met Capesius, who became interested in her whole method of contacting the spiritual world so that she often came to his own house, where she met Strader. He also became absorbed in her revelations and finally felt that he could not do without her, as her visions so confirmed one another that he became utterly convinced of the spiritual world. Without any hope of fulfilment he consulted her for advice on how to face his problem. Theodora feels that when heart speaks to heart the paths of destiny become clear and so they were brought together.

Strader then speaks of all she has meant to him during these seven years. She has brought him new life and strength so that he now sees that even in technical work, by those who are aware of it, spiritual meaning can be found. However, we now hear that Theodora's visionary gifts have gradually disappeared and Strader wonders whether this is not a great pain to her, although she has seemed calm and tranquil.

Theodora replies that she can patiently accept what the spirit world dictates so that her loss of vision has been no grief to her, but now it is returning in a way that is terrible and is giving her cause for great anxiety, as she can only hate what is revealed. She feels that some dark power is trying to approach her and her struggle to keep it at bay is bringing about a great loss of strength. When she summoned all her forces together to ask the spirit world for revelation as to the cause of this haunting, there appeared before her the figure of Thomasius.

Strader is deeply shocked. He has always striven to admire Thomasius, but when he now remembers what happened in front of the Rosicrucian Brotherhood he is filled with doubt.

At this moment he observes that Theodora has passed over into a trance state. He cries out in alarm to her to know what it is she is now seeing.

Here the scene ends.

This scene well illustrates how helpful it is when two characters of different backgrounds and ways of thought come together. Strader and Theodora are creating new karma. Her connection with the Baldes is a renewing of their life in the Middle Ages after she had been deserted by her father and they had adopted her. Capesius, who in that incarnation had abandoned her, is in this life anxious to understand the sources of her spiritual visions. Celia (Theodora) and her brother Thomas the Miner (Johannes/Thomasius) were prevented through the discovery of their blood bond from coming together in marriage. Celia accepted the situation and showed wisdom in her understanding of their father, but Thomas was set in his hostility and feeling of personal grievance. The pain he caused her was a forewarning of what is now happening in the present life.

Scene Five
THE BALDES' COTTAGE
We learn that Theodora has died and Strader has come for consolation to the Baldes, who loved her dearly. Capesius is present but he appears to take no notice of his companions or their conversation. Felix attempts to console Strader by speaking of how they can still meet Theodora in their thoughts; but he himself expresses surprise at her early death. When meeting people he has often been granted a vision of their life powers and knowledge of whether they will be able to fulfil their life span or will meet an early death. On account of Theodora's tranquil and happy nature he was certain that she had many years still to live and is surprised at his failure to perceive the truth.

This confession leads Strader to describe Theodora's last illness. He speaks of how she lost her radiance and became deeply troubled. She felt that an adverse power was haunting her and trying to obtain possession of her. She struggled against this and when she called together all her forces to find what it was that pursued her, the image of Thomasius always appeared before her.

At this moment Capesius suddenly seems to wake up. He declares that by a decree of fate Thomasius and Theodora must never come together in sensual passion. Thomasius is disobeying this occult law and giving himself over to powers of darkness. According to destiny, Maria should be the guide of Thomasius. He left her for a time and has therefore come under the spell of Lucifer, who has led him to a wrongful passion for Theodora. Capesius now reveals what we have already learned from Scene Three, that Lucifer summoned the soul of Theodora to appear before Thomasius and wakened in the latter's Double this evil longing. It is this which has caused Theodora all the pain and brought about her death.

Strader is deeply distressed at what he feels a cruel fate and asks Felix whether he can believe Capesius or not. Felix now describes what he has observed lately in Capesius. Most of the time he seems unwilling to take part in earthly affairs, as we have already gathered from Scene Three. Consequently he lives in a kind of trance and only performs the necessary daily deeds out of habit. He regularly visits his old friends but he sits with them without taking interest in what they do or say. Felicia adds, however, that if some word refers to spiritual truths, Capesius will suddenly awaken and say something relevant to their conversation. Felix confirms that as far as he can judge whatever Capesius contributes seems to be valid. But Strader is still uncertain what to do.

At this moment the soul of Theodora appears. She says

that Thomasius is caught in this evil power of Lucifer, but those who know him must not leave him to succumb. Maria has already made a strong vow and Theodora herself will pour forth blessing from the source of love so that he can be recalled. She then turns to Strader and especially addresses him. She describes how Thomasius has powers of seership and will therefore be able to follow her into the spirit world, but this must at all costs be prevented. Here she speaks of their need for Strader's help. He is deeply moved by her turning to him as she used to do in their life together on earth. But she now signifies that he must turn to Capesius, and Felix explains that he must listen to what it is that Capesius has to say.

Capesius describes how in order to follow Theodora into the spirit world Thomasius will have to develop still further powers. But he is under the spell of Lucifer and whatever he acquires will in reality become Lucifer's possession. Thomasius will be filled with a longing to drain Theodora's spiritual light, but he does not realise that this will then be taken over by Lucifer, who longs to deprive the good gods of what is due to them. Lucifer also will be able to turn the scientific work which Thomasius has achieved to evil ends. He will deprive it of its true influence and bring it into his own power. In this realm Strader can be of help. If he can transform his human knowledge so that it will express spiritual ideals then this will divert Lucifer's aim, but to this end Strader will need to become a pupil of Benedictus.

Strader again asks Felix whether he can rely on all that Capesius has told him and Felix explains more fully what he has already related. He says that Capesius is really destined to fulfil a high spiritual calling, but because he has rather evaded his true task and become too much caught up in modern materialistic thinking he has not sufficiently prepared himself to this end. Consequently certain experiences are being bestowed upon him as preparation. He is able to receive certain visions of the spiritual world, and the Guardian of the Threshold has received orders to allow him to pass through at times into the spirit kingdom; but owing to his lack of realising the true nature of thinking Capesius cannot remain there, the gates close against him. Capesius is so often absent when the conversation concerns only earthly affairs because he is living really in his spiritual visions.

Felicia now adds that there is one link between human speech and his supersensible experiences and that is when she tells him fairy stories. She observed when he felt exhausted and dried out with his everyday teaching, he used to come to her for refreshment and her stories gave him new life. They raised him from the earthly level to that world he really wanted to know. She will now try to help him by speaking inwardly her stories so that he may be able to carry them over into the spirit world.

In his previous life in the fourteenth century, Capesius had failed in regard to his connection with Thomasius and Theodora. He is now striving to put right what he lacked and this gives him the impulse to wish to help them now on their further path. Hence he is urged to speak to Felix and Strader of what is needed to save Thomasius and prevent his further harming of Theodora. Theodora herself, in spite of deep suffering caused by Thomasius, is nevertheless prepared to pour down blessing from the source of love in order to aid him.

Scene Six
We are here presented with the Etheric World where we see

all that is living and moving behind the realm of the senses which appears to us in daily life. We are shown plant forms in perpetual motion, and storms and turmoil frequently disturb the scene. Maria and Capesius are present.

In this sphere Capesius hears the resounding words of Benedictus which he had meditated long ago, as is described in the first scene of *The Soul's Probation*. He cannot understand why words which were spoken for pupils on earth should resound in the Etheric World, as he considers that earthly thoughts have no meaning here. In reality Benedictus, later with the help of Maria, is leading Capesius in an important step forward in his development, for the latter has never been able to recognise the reality of thinking. He imagines that he himself creates his own thoughts, whereas in truth the thoughts themselves are present in the spirit world and become apparent only to those who have learned to understand what it is that the sense world represents. If we think truly we allow the phenomena of the sense world to reveal to us their origin and significance. Capesius feels at home in the Etheric World and he cannot understand the essential being of what has been created in the physical world, but when he re-enters the physical world he is bewildered by the single objects which he meets; he feels himself plunged into darkness.

Maria realises that Benedictus is leading her through an important stage of her development, for in the Etheric World the language we speak in everyday life has no meaning, words have become mere symbols. Benedictus is able to bring in mantric form meaning that still lives in the Etheric World. She will lay aside her earthly thinking and give herself up to what he has to tell her. Then when she comes back into earthly life and meditates, there will awake in her again what she understood in the Etheric World.

Benedictus now appears.

Capesius cannot understand why Benedictus should need to bring words that belong to earthly life into the spirit land. What can they mean here? In reply Benedictus describes how for those who have entered his circle, whether consciously or unconsciously, he must henceforth take responsibility and follow their future development. Capesius again complains that he does not want to hear his name spoken. Benedictus tells Capesius that the latter does not want to feel himself enclosed in a physical body, but he must learn to understand it otherwise he will never realise himself truly as a being. He has learned to free himself from his body and from the dream life of thinking, but he is too weak to wander into the spirit land in full confidence and too much caught in the spirit world to face the darkness of earthly life. Though he is free from his earthly body he is not yet free from the kind of thinking which he has known on earth and so cannot see himself in his true being. He will only find the world truly real when he has learned to view his thinking as outside himself, just as the seer has to behold his body as something apart. He must learn to look at his thoughts as image pictures and then, through the force of seership which he has already acquired, change them into living knowledge. The thoughts which have shaped themselves in space will then become beings that mirror human thinking.

As Capesius and Maria leave the stage, Philia, Astrid and Luna appear in a gleaming cloud. They call to the thinker that through active will, wakened feeling and controlled thinking he should bring his dreams to life.

Lucifer and Ahriman appear with the spirits who serve them. They take up Benedictus' words from the Book of Life, but distort them, and the beings that serve them carry these out in eurythmy so that Capesius is able to realise thoughts being brought into movement.

Philia, Astrid and Luna repeat their former words but with a change into the past tense, because they realise that Capesius has awakened to a certain recognition that thoughts, feelings and will impulses are there in the Etheric World and are not created by the human being. He wonders why people fall into such illusions, but he does not know where to find the answer. He fears that if he asks Lucifer the answer will still be illusory.

Maria now comes to Capesius' aid. We need to remember that in the third scene Capesius claimed that she owed him a karmic debt because she, as the Monk in the 14th century, had stolen away from him his possibility of a relationship with his son Thomas the Miner (Johannes/Thomasius). She tells him to look for his answer in the abyss, but this gives him fear. Lucifer states that he is the giver of beauty to man and Maria points out that fear does not belong to Lucifer. Capesius must look in quite another direction. Lucifer explains that it is he who awakens the creative impulses in human beings. If it were not for his inspiration men would remain cold and unfeeling. But behind Lucifer's words lies the implication contained in the phrase 'men think they should hate me' because in reality Lucifer's gift of creativity often brings illusions and separates human beings from one another.

Ahriman now speaks of his gift to man. He bestows upon him strength. He planned to give man power to equal the gods but the gods themselves refused this and so Ahriman has been cast down into lower regions. It is he who makes man believe that the physical world is the only reality, and it is this outlook which denies spiritual origin, which gives man fear. Capesius realises that anyone who recognises these two powers learns the way to seek and find both fear and hate; and Benedictus shows him that he must now find himself in cosmic thoughts as these will confirm for him his own existence. Capesius at last feels that he has found himself again.

At this point we hear the story resound that Felicia is speaking inwardly for Capesius to hear in the Etheric World. What she describes has a relationship with his own condition. He himself would like to be similar to the Child of Light but he has not hitherto found the impulse to wish to come to the help of suffering human beings. The story in a way is a delicate reflection of the Christian path. The Child of Light finds joy in helping man but has himself to face scorn and derision. This Capesius has not previously had the courage to do. It is a picture really of the forces he must awaken in himself.

Philia, Astrid and Luna again appear. Philia calls upon the soul to experience itself in the light of cosmic expanses, Astrid summons the spirit to overcome fear and Luna shows how the one who aspires to spirit heights must find a firm foundation within himself. They are followed, however, by the Other Philia, who though seeming to agree with them nevertheless introduces a Luciferic temptation. She speaks of awakening glad senses within the human being which will lead to the region of the gods that give radiant beauty to souls. These words of the Other Philia give the warning that Capesius will still be in danger of sometimes succumbing to Luciferic influences.

Scene Seven
Now for the first time we meet with the Guardian of the Threshold. Thomasius has had a partial encounter with the Lesser Guardian through his Double, but he

is now forcefully demanding spiritual experiences for which he is entirely unfit.

Maria has already shown in Scene Two that she is familiar with the Guardian. She prepared herself, as related in *The Soul's Probation*, by renouncing her personal love for Thomasius. After her vision into the Middle Ages she is able to withstand Ahriman's wiles. In the second scene of *The Guardian of the Threshold* in her words of encouragement to Thomasius, she describes the true task of human beings on earth. On that account she will be able to accompany him into the ever empty fields of ice where the human soul must learn to create new light amid the darkness of death.

In this scene we are in the Astral World, which is shown as being full of the disturbances caused by people's egoistic ambitions and desires. The Guardian stands at the entrance to the Spirit Land, refusing entry to those who are inspired by selfish aims, as they will experience only illusions and create confusion. If they then return to the physical world they will do great damage to their own being. He allows only those to pass him who have attained complete serenity of soul.

Thomasius and Maria appear. Thomasius claims right of entry because he is no longer the same being who inhabited the earthly body of Johannes/Thomasius. He once lived in the illusion that his artistic creations were true revelations of the spirit but he came to realise that he was only spinning out of his own feeling life. He thought he had experienced the blissfulness of supersensible knowledge and in his relationship with Maria, which he had imagined was entirely spiritual, he was led to recognise with horror its true source. He learned to discover that in general it was the bonds of blood that really led people together and these relationships

THE GUARDIAN OF THE THRESHOLD 87

were carried over into a future incarnation. Hence he had come to suspect the desires which tried to raise the human being into the spiritual world. This striving bound the soul to earth more firmly than a normal daily life. Therefore he felt the need to learn from Lucifer, for it is only the gods who can approach man in their reality. Now it is important for him to find the soul which Lucifer has led to him, and with the strength and determination bestowed by Lucifer he demands an entry to the spirit world, for he knows that Theodora is beyond this threshold.

The Guardian warns Thomasius that he has cast away the work he had done in scientific thinking and hence bequeathed it to Ahriman. He is now under the leadership of Lucifer and all that Lucifer has given him will disappear beyond the Threshold, so that he will become completely void and empty. Thomasius, however, demands entry, for he says he will receive his light from Theodora and that will be sufficient for him.

At this moment Maria intervenes. She knows that the Guardian has to refuse entry to all who have not attained maturity and renounced all earthly egoism. But she herself claims the right to guide Thomasius because she has prepared herself for this. She made a vow before the throne of Lucifer that she would serve love in such a way that no harm could come through it either now or in future ages, for it was entirely selfless. Long ago she came to Thomasius as a messenger of Christ and brought him to a true understanding of the Christian impulse. He will no longer listen to her on earth, but he will have to listen to what she speaks to him in the spirit world.

Thomasius now perceives a being who claims his attention. He describes to Maria that he sees a dignified old man passing through a crowd of people who make way for him in deep reverence. He becomes aware that this old man has occupied himself deeply with spiritual thought for he has had a teacher inspired by love and wisdom through initiates. He longs to know more about him. When he asks Maria if she can see this old man she explains that she can see him only through Thomasius and she realises that he has something very special to communicate.

Thomasius says that the old man has now faded from his sight but he can hear the conversation of all those in the crowd. They describe how the old man was once a valiant warrior with ambition to be first in the field. He committed many cruelties in his determination to lead; but then a reverse of fortune caused his overthrow and he had to retire in disgrace. From this time onwards he hated his fellow men and longed to have his revenge. But at last he realised the impossibility of this and he joined a small circle who strove to understand spiritual wisdom, and so he became renowned as a holy man. Thomasius is filled with most powerful love and desire to know this character more fully, whether he is on earth now or not.

Maria reminds him that many people on earth today, if they looked back and saw their previous incarnations, would be filled with shame at what they have now become. Is Thomasius so sure that this character must stand on the same high peak now that he did long ago? Thomasius is indignant that Maria is casting doubt on his enthusiasm and asks if thoughts in this region have a different meaning from what they had in earthly life.

The Guardian warns Thomasius that what has appeared before him is to be a probation for his own soul. He must look down into the deeper layers of his being which he has never consciously wished to do. He must find what is hidden there as he is living in blindness. The one whom he seeks with such feverish love will appear in his reality and he will then see who it is that he loves most strongly.

Lucifer now calls to Thomasius to learn the strength of love which will hold him upright in the progress of the world. This recalls to Thomasius the thoughts of Theodora, and he imagines that what he has experienced must be her in one of her previous incarnations, and it is she whom he loves the best.

The Guardian tells him he will have to face what he has demanded. He will learn who it is that he really loves best and find if it brings to him the experience which he has imagined. The scene closes with the Other Philia calling to Thomasius not to listen to the Guardian because he is too remote from life and too austere. He has no idea that human suffering can be eased only through earthly love.

Scene Eight
AHRIMAN'S KINGDOM
We see a dark gorge with granite rocks, out of which appear skeletons. Ahriman is standing on a rocky slope and Hilary and Frederick Trautman (Romanus) enter. Trautman is troubled because although their holy book says that this place is good, he feels there is something terrible about it. But Hilary reassures him that the seed has to fall in the ground and die in order that new life may emerge. Trautman complains that if it were not for the statement in their holy book, he would feel that this realm was evil. On the other hand, Hilary's natural feelings tell him that all is well.

Ahriman now speaks to Hilary and Trautman in a disguised voice so that they do not recognise him. He tells them that all Thomasius was able to offer them of any value had been inspired by him. If now they give their hopes to Strader then Ahriman himself will be able to give a right guidance, for he is in control of all that concerns nature powers and their knowledge in this sphere has been lacking.

Trautman now confesses to Hilary that he is deeply troubled. He has hitherto tried to suppress any criticisms as their Order has demanded obedience to their superiors; and he has gladly accepted the guidance of Hilary's higher wisdom. But recently he has found that Hilary has been gravely wrong in many of his judgments and events have proved that he has not given right guidance. Trautman feels himself oppressed by a kind of nightmare with his deep concern.

Hilary accepts this mildly and says that they must wait for the spirit to give guidance about what path they should next follow.

Ahriman mockingly comments that if Hilary and Trautman really recognised him they would not dream of coming to him and would utterly condemn any who came to him for advice.

We can see from the conversation that Hilary is still living in the old traditions of the Rosicrucian Brotherhood. He is patiently waiting for the spirit to give guidance, but he does not realise that the time has come when a new step forward can be made only through the spiritual activity of human beings. Trautman is more realistic but he also does not know the way in which to find a new step forward, although he recognises that in the kingdom of Ahriman he is meeting with malevolent forces.

There now enter Strader and the twelve characters who were offered admittance to the Rosicrucian Brotherhood.

Ahriman is seeking to bind these more closely to the one who was closely connected with them in the Middle

Ages. He hopes in this way to be able to master Strader's work and use it for his own ends. Strader is surprised that Benedictus has sent him to this place to cultivate his powers of thought. He has imagined he would enter lofty spiritual realms and he realises that this is a kingdom of the dead. When Ahriman assures him that he can learn wisdom here, Strader asks what being he is addressing, and why he is led together with these twelve people. Ahriman tells him that these are here only as sleeping souls, but they will reveal all unaware their inner thoughts and feelings.

The twelve characters speak in a dream-like way, somewhat differently from their utterances in waking life. Frederick Geist, Michael Edelmann and George Wahrmund are almost euphoric in their enthusiasm for spiritual knowledge. On the other hand, those who have advised caution are more closely bound to the life of every day. Ferdinand Reinecke declares the first aim should be for man to seek what profits himself, while Maria Treufels considers Strader is the one who will give new hope to the Mystic League, as only a sharp sense of reality will bring spirit wisdom. Ahriman makes mocking comments to Strader about each in turn. He says that he needs twelve to represent the many different points of view of men on earth but there is no need for more as the thirteenth would only reflect what one of the twelve has already given him. We see that Ahriman counts human beings only so far as numbers are concerned. He has no interest in human individuality. If he can obtain power over twelve, he can spare Lucifer five so long as he has seven for himself. At this point he covers Strader's ears so that he may not hear and confesses that he has not yet succeeded but that he will go on struggling throughout all eternity.

Ahriman now assures Strader that in his realm he will

hear the truth and if he wishes only for inspiring ideas he must go to other beings. Even the gods need him because without him there would be no true thinking and men would only dream their way into higher worlds. Strader at first feels that he could serve Ahriman, for only lack of common sense would rouse opposition. What Ahriman offers seems to him good, as it gives strength and only if men are evil could it be turned to a wrong account. Even Ahriman's mockery could have a healthy effect on making men recognise their failings. Suddenly he realises that he has uttered words which on earth would seem to him untrue. What Ahriman says is true only for this realm and human thoughts freeze here and can go no further. He senses behind Ahriman's words a feeling of pain which also gives him pain, and beholding Ahriman he is moved to weep.

Strader leaves the stage and Maria and Thomasius enter.

Thomasius is at once filled with fear. He does not know where to find the strength to bear it. Maria calls to him to feel her solemn holy vow. Its healing influence will give him the necessary power.

Ahriman realises that Benedictus has sent them to him. He tells Thomasius that the Guardian had to send him into this realm to find the light in the depths of his own nature, for Ahriman can give truth, but always with pain such as he himself has suffered for countless ages, because in this realm truth has to separate itself from joy. Wishes can bring happiness only when accompanied by soul warmth but here all wishes freeze. Maria declares that she must lead her friend into the ever empty fields of ice where human spirits have to create new light amid the darkness, where the powers of life are lamed. She calls on Thomasius to put forth his full strength.

THE GUARDIAN OF THE THRESHOLD 93

The Guardian now appears. He tells Thomasius that the soul he saw in a form in which it had lived many years ago is the one which in the depths of his heart he loves the most. Soul pictures are illusions when born out of desire. Thomasius will confront the one to whom he is most devoted. Thomasius now once more beholds the image of the old man and asks why he conceals himself. The form begins to change. As Thomasius cries out that it must be Theodora, his Double appears and he realises that the one he loves the best is in reality himself. The Double calls out to Thomasius 'Know what I am... behold yourself in me'; however Maria affirms that she will accompany her friend to cosmic depths where out of utter loss souls who recognise the spirit can create new life.

Scene Nine
A SUNNY MORNING LANDSCAPE with signs in the distance of an industrial city.

After the dramatic events of Ahriman's kingdom we now experience a period of quiet calm. Capesius, Strader and Thomasius have withstood their trials and are now ready to take on their true tasks.

At first Capesius, while alone, speaks of what he owes to Benedictus. In this setting Benedictus has often gathered his pupils around him, for the beauty of nature has opened their souls to receive his spirit wisdom; while in the dark city their leader goes to ease the suffering of the many who labour in the darkness.

Capesius speaks of the wonderful way in which Benedictus guided him through the spirit world and brought him to realise his own true being.

At this moment Benedictus joins Capesius and explains to him that through his spirit progress and the deeds of others in the circle of his students the misunderstandings of a past life have been solved and they are now ready to take up their true tasks. All that Capesius has experienced will enable him to find his true helpers and serve the path of progress that Benedictus himself guards.

Capesius now knows that he can trust Benedictus' leadership, and he perceives the tasks to which his future must be devoted. Benedictus explains to Capesius that in future he, Thomasius and Strader will need to form a trinity, working together. It becomes clear in this scene that a particular power is created by certain groups coming together. There is a special strength* in a triad which the three single members could not achieve apart. We can see this in legends and history. The Egyptian myth of Osiris and Isis requires for its fulfilment the presence of Horus. In Greek times, the whole of philosophy was founded on the passing on from one to the other of the thought of Socrates, Plato and Aristotle.

Capesius now understands why his destiny, which had seemed so incomprehensible, has led him in so fortunate a way. Though he had studied Benedictus' philosophy for many years, he had never understood the thoughts as more than theories, and when their spirit truth suddenly lighted up he became confused and unable to unite the two approaches to life.

Benedictus implies that whereas the general approach to the Guardian of the Threshold is through disciplined spirit progress, in Capesius' case it had happened differently. He had seen beyond the Threshold in glimpses before he had attained a fully disciplined understanding.

At this point Strader appears and Capesius leaves them.

*See second half of lecture 5, 'The Secrets of the Threshold', eight lectures, Munich, 24th—31st August, 1913, Rudolf Steiner Press, London.

Strader explains his pain on finding himself in the kingdom of Ahriman. But the memory of his last incarnation in medieval times has wakened up in him and he remembers his relationship with the Templar Order and with the twelve peasants. Benedictus explains to him Ahriman's intentions to unite the twelve with him for future lives. A genuine soul bond has been woven between Strader himself and the twelve, but the latter must be aware of this so that Ahriman does not have power over them. Benedictus now explains how in earthly life there has to be an understanding of measure and number. There is a reality in the working together of twelve followers, not as Ahriman pictures, merely as an abstract number, but because when the twelve different points of view are brought together in a group of people who understand one another and are willing to work together, then new powers can be liberated. We see this in the history of many movements, for instance Jacob's twelve sons create the twelve tribes of Israel; Christ was followed by his twelve disciples; in the cult of Arthur's Court of the Round Table there were twelve knights who represented the twelve signs of the Zodiac. In working with the material world it is essential for Strader to understand Ahriman but not to be bound by him. Strader is confident now that he will be able to rescue his work from Ahriman's domain.

They leave the scene and Maria and Thomasius approach. It is clear from Maria's opening words that Thomasius has now passed the Guardian, for she affirms that he has conquered and brought truth out of the realms of ice, so that he will no longer want to create in wishful dreams. Thomasius recognises that he has been indulging in unlawful desires without any reference to reality and he now feels that Maria and Benedictus have brought to him a higher life.

Maria also speaks to him about the importance of measure and number though it does not emerge quite so explicitly, but it is shown that between the necessities of the physical world and the truth of spirit life there has to be a balanced power and of this we hear more in the next scene. Thomasius realises that he has a twofold being and he is determined now that his lower being shall not interfere with his spiritual tasks.

Scene Ten
THE TEMPLE OF THE ROSICRUCIAN BROTHERHOOD
In this scene we have a fulfilment of the closing one of the first drama *The Portal of Initiation*. There Johannes had an imaginative vision of what could be attained one day in the distant future if certain characters were able to develop their innate potentials. He himself, Capesius and Strader have now attained a level at which they are able to unite with those who have hitherto carried the spiritual wisdom to guide mankind. Hence the Temple of the Sun which had appeared to him in the spiritual world is now fully established on earth.

In the East stand Benedictus and Hilary; in the South Bellicosus and Torquatus; in the West Trautman. Benedictus explains that his pupils have made progress in receiving the light in their own way so that they will be able to share it with one another. But this can happen rightfully only if they are aware of the harmony in measure and number so that thereby they can form a higher unity in this sacred place. They are now standing at the threshold of this Temple, where their separate natures can unite in accordance with the decree of cosmic destiny. In this way they will bring something new to what has become old, although until now it has been nobly guarded. Hence, as his pupils have prepared themselves through their different probations, he is about to introduce them to the Brotherhood. He assures them that these new leaders will honour the holy rites. They are called by cosmic destiny to fulfil these positions for a certain time and then in due course when they exhaust their strength others will succeed them. Benedictus now refers to the time when Thomasius through an unconscious recognition that he could not cross this Threshold until he had passed the Guardian, refused to accept their invitation to unite with them. Now, however, he returns to them having achieved the necessary standard.

Hilary recognises that Benedictus has acted according to cosmic destiny and humbly accepts the guidance that is flowing through the spirit. They are ready to welcome the pupils to take over the leadership.

Thomasius, Capesius, Strader, Maria, Felix and Felicia Balde are now admitted. Trautman and Torquatus lead them to their places, Thomasius in front of Hilary and Benedictus, Capesius to the south and Strader to the west. The other newcomers take their stand in the centre.

Hilary greets Thomasius with the warning that only truth can be spoken in this holy place. Any untruth would incur guilt for the speaker and great grief for the spirit world. He himself has done his best to serve the Mystic League and he is now prepared to hand over his key of office with his blessing to Thomasius.

Thomasius receives the words of Hilary with humility. In his own personality he knows that he is completely unworthy to cross this Threshold but powers of fate have willed it. Benedictus and Maria have awakened in him his higher being. In serving this Mystic League he must never allow his lower self to interfere with his sacred duty, which is to serve the progress of the earth. With regard to his own weaknesses, he must work upon himself in private. His higher self will not be fully developed until the far future, but it is capable, with the aid of the spirit, of guiding the Temple's sacred tasks.

Torquatus welcomes Capesius as one who, owing to his recent experiences with Lucifer, is well able to fulfil what is required here, where love should illuminate wisdom. However, he warns him that Lucifer is ever ready to steal upon him unseen.

Capesius feels that he understands Lucifer well, for the spirit who brought wisdom to mankind is in himself neither good nor bad. Only those who misuse his gifts turn his influence to evil. Torquatus replies that Capesius is considering only the effects of Lucifer but not his real being. One cannot understand Lucifer by mere reasoning. The seer needs to evaluate with love the powers at work in the universe and turn them to good.

Benedictus now outlines the part to be played by Maria. As love speaks with a gentle voice it might easily be unrecognised. Maria, owing to the selflessness of her vow before Lucifer, will be able to radiate love in support of the three who are to work together and thus strengthen the necessary threefold harmony of cosmic law.

Maria explains that the words which Capesius spoke are of such depth that they can be understood only by those who serve love in the light of the spirit. They could easily be distorted by evil minds and lead astray. Lucifer, as the bearer of the light, rays forth wisdom and wakens man's joy in the beauty of the sense world. But this is accompanied by a most powerful feeling of self. Man has need of that other Spirit Who selflessly expresses His Being in the glory of the world but whose highest gift is when He lives within man's own being and in His love transforms death into life. Man can behold Lucifer's beauty but should never allow him to enter into his will. He should confront him with the words: 'Not I, but the Christ in me'.

Benedictus confirms that Maria as the bearer of the Christ is able to bring light into the Temple through the Divine loving wisdom of the Redeemer. In a previous life she estranged the son Thomas the Miner (Thomasius) from his father the First Preceptor (Capesius); now she brings the son back to the father and through the power of the Christ has cancelled her debt.

The speeches of Benedictus and Maria are in reality the culminating point of the whole drama, as it is only through Christ that the balance can truly be kept between Lucifer and Ahriman; and we can see in future developments that Thomasius and Capesius are still liable to temptations from Lucifer and Strader has to struggle with Ahriman.

Magnus Bellicosus (Gairman) welcomes Felix and Felicia Balde. He shows that the time has come when spiritual powers pour down wisdom on those who do not necessarily belong to any occult group. It is important now that the Mystic League should unite these impulses. Felicia modestly explains that her only gift of spirit wisdom is her ability to tell fairy tales and she has had to rely on Capesius to realise their truth. For this reason she accepts their invitation to unite with the Rosicrucian Brotherhood.

Felix Balde describes how for a long time he sought spirit wisdom in solitude and was often able to experience the presence of supersensible powers. Recently he has received presentiments that it would be right to unite himself with others. He even had a vision of a temple, which he here sees expressed in earthly form.

Trautman (Romanus) welcomes Strader to succeed him

and describes the latter's influence like the setting sun in contrast to the rising rays of Thomasius. It was necessary for him to meet with Ahriman in order to experience the strength of his own thinking in contrast to Ahriman's dead thoughts. He has to recognise that words are only images of divine powers.

Strader acknowledges that for a long time he was able to realise the light only through its reflections. But then for seven years the spirit was revealed to him (through Theodora) and showed him that his previous thinking was indeed only frozen so that he stood in doubt of everything. But now he knows that the spirit light must grow so strongly within him that it will shine through all eternity so that he can find his true goals and blessing can flow from his creative work. At this moment Theodora becomes visible as a spirit being and tells him that because he strove towards her light, at the right time she was allowed to gain the light for him. And Strader assures her, as his spirit messenger, her light will shine on all the words which he speaks in this place, for she too is consecrated to this holy service.

At this moment the three soul powers and the Other Philia appear in a cloud of light. The Other Philia shows herself completely transformed. She describes how the aspiring souls and spirits are soaring up from the world of form and are being granted grace of light by the divine powers.

Philia promises that she will pray the cosmic powers to ray out their light so that what has been awakened here will never be extinguished.

Astrid will bestow love and warmth on those here present so that the mood of consecration can be sustained.

Luna appeals to the primal powers to give courage and

strength so that deeds of self-sacrifice which now seem temporal can be transformed for all eternity.

THE SOULS' AWAKENING

Foreword

Some time has passed since the events of the third play; Harry Collison reckons this to be about a year. Now we find that the members of the Rosicrucian Brotherhood who previously had kept their spiritual knowledge and their everyday lives distinctly separate, realise that outer deeds should spring from spiritual knowledge. Hilary, who was in a former incarnation the Grand Master of the Templar Order, is now in outer life the head of a factory for the making of furniture and other articles, but this play illustrates the fact that it is no easy task to bring spiritual knowledge into the realms which depend very largely for their success on traditions from the past. It is difficult to bring new designs and new methods immediately into effective action.

In *The Guardian of the Threshold* Johannes/Thomasius, Capesius and Strader achieved a certain development which enabled them to work together with understanding and they are now summoned by Hilary to take over the leadership of his factory, but only too soon the struggle to bring their lofty ideals into a practical sphere begins to cause difficulties. We find that once again Johannes/Thomasius and Capesius tend to yield to their former weaknesses.

After Rudolf Steiner's death the same situation arose with many of the practical ventures that had been launched during the last years of his life. Completely new faculties had to be developed in order to bring about a new social order and new styles of artistic creation. Owing to the very highly intellectual civilisation into which these efforts were being introduced, the public at large was sceptical of these new ideas. It almost seems as though Rudolf Steiner in 1913 at the time when these plays were produced, was prophetically aware of this.

Whereas the first two plays reveal chiefly the development of Johannes/Thomasius and *The Guardian of the Threshold* that of Capesius, this play is chiefly concerned with the progress of Strader.

Scene One
THE OFFICE IN HILARY'S FACTORY furnished in a conventional style.

The Manager and the secretary are discussing the many complaints they have been receiving about the unsatisfactory quality of the work and the unpunctuality of the delivery of articles. Hilary's family had built up a very successful and highly esteemed enterprise and it would seem that the concern is beginning to lose its good name. When Hilary enters, the Manager asks for a private conversation with him and complains of the general dissatisfaction. He laments to Hilary that he is making a great mistake in trying to introduce spiritual conceptions into the activities of daily life. Hilary seems unmoved as he is convinced of the power of the spirit to make its impact upon the world and for a while he is assured of his ability to persuade the Manager of the ultimate success of his plans to bring in Johannes/Thomasius as Artistic Designer and Strader as the adviser for the technical side of the work. The Manager, however, believes that those who have developed their spiritual life are led into illusions if they try to bring it into their daily work. He therefore has no confidence in these people and declares that if Hilary follows this path he himself will have to retire. Hilary is deeply shaken as the Manager has always been his standby, but he still feels that a conversation with Strader will bring about a change of heart.

At this moment Strader enters. He recognises that the Manager has no confidence in him because of his previous failure with regard to his mechanical invention but assures him that through what he has learned he will now be able to progress. Strader then makes a statement which becomes a leading motif of his development during this play: 'and yet what comes will have to come about'. This shows that he is now aware that spiritual powers take up the hopes and deeds of human beings and these can come to maturity only when the time is ripe.

Scene Two
A MOUNTAIN LANDSCAPE WITH A WATERFALL
Hilary's house can be seen in the background. Johannes is yielding to the beauty of the scene around him and giving himself up to dreaming of artistic creation. Capesius, unseen by Johannes, is sitting in the background.

Johannes feels that his recent progress in spiritual consciousness is hindering him from the gift which he had in the past of being inspired as an artist by the beauty of the sense world. He would like to abandon all that he has recently attained, and is indulging in feelings for Maria which he had long ago, and which should now have been overcome.

At this moment Maria appears as a thought form of Johannes and he is shocked by her expression of stern reproach. He wishes to see Maria as she used to be before she had transformed him and led him to awake consciousness, which he feels kills his artistic nature. He would like to be as he was as a young artist many years ago and feels that his reawakened self is robbing him of his creative gifts.

Maria warns him that the picture he has created of her has no relation to the truth. He is weaving in illusions. This is disturbing her own spiritual calm. He must learn to recognise this lower self and then it will disappear.

Johannes realises that she is speaking the truth and that he should make efforts to overcome this lazy giving way to dreams. Nevertheless that early stage of life which he should have left behind has a compelling power; although he knows he should renounce it, he is still filled with longing.

Benedictus appears by the side of Maria. He summons Johannes to recognise the call of his true being. He must ever bear in mind the higher self which he has gradually to attain. We are reminded of Johannes' own speech in the last scene of *The Guardian of the Threshold* where he himself recognises his twofold nature and acknowledges that he must always strive for his higher being to be active in the world while he struggles inwardly with his own weaknesses.

Maria now calls upon the holy earnest vow which she affirmed before Lucifer in *The Guardian of the Threshold*. She tells Johannes that he must seek her in the ever empty fields of ice where human beings can create out of nothingness. Her strength is given to him to aid him in this task, but he must never seek to contact her in illusory dreams of the past. Johannes, however, feels too strongly the impulse to live in his dreams. He is not interested in facing the abyss where awake consciousness has to be developed, and prefers to abandon the spiritual heights in order to be an artistic creator.

Capesius in the meantime has experienced Johannes' inner struggle and now approaches him. He is deeply disturbed at what he has seen and wonders whether it is truth or illusion. He has heard from Benedictus that the experience of another's inner soul life can be an important step forward in spirit vision and imagines that if this is the case it is a call to him to develop his seership rather than undertake external works. When he tells Johannes, who appears disturbed at his approach, that he has felt very near to him, Johannes shudders and Capesius realises that he has seen truly.

Maria, who has felt Johannes' conflict of soul, approaches him and is surprised to find Capesius, as she has imagined that the latter is satisfied with Hilary's proposals. When Capesius declares that a sign has shown him he must withdraw, she reproves him, as spiritual vision should never interfere with earthly duties. She also points out to him that his teaching within the group that Hilary has called together cannot hinder his progress because he will be working within the realm of his own spiritual research. However, he replies that the bringing of spiritual knowledge into words and concepts can kill it and therefore he is no longer prepared to follow this path.

Lucifer appears and triumphantly warns Maria that her gift of love will be in vain and will fall under his power, for both these souls are now caught up in their own egoistic wishes, which play into his hands.

Capesius is convinced that he must follow his path in solitude and he is drawn to consider Felix Balde as his example as the latter has always developed his spiritual wisdom in his own particular way. With these words he departs.

Maria tells Johannes that she sees this as a stroke of

destiny, for Capesius has fallen into a spirit sleep, and until he awakens he will be unable to undertake his task. Now she and Johannes must bind themselves more strongly to the work in hand. Johannes declares that he is quite incapable of carrying this venture. Like Capesius he too must sink into a spirit sleep. In the future when he wakens he will be able to work for the spirit, but not at present, for it is he who drove away Capesius by revealing to him unconsciously his own dreaming into his long suppressed lower being.

Maria now assures Johannes that she has been instructed by the spirit to tell him that elemental beings are approaching. He knows of these but has never consciously allied himself with them; and recognition will awaken in him memories of times long past. As they are creative in the world of nature he is really closely connected with them and they will open his eyes to the power with which he has been working and bring him self-knowledge. Johannes draws together his forces and declares he will defy the temptations of his lower being.

Gnomes and Sylphs now appear in the foreground. The Gnomes relate how they have been active since long before man had self-consciousness. They are outstandingly clever in knowing all that is happening in regard to the relationship of the earth and the starry worlds. They cannot understand why human beings do not know everything as they do and therefore mock their stupid, stumbling thoughts.

Philia, Astrid, Luna and the Other Philia now appear.

The Sylphs are concerned with the becoming and fading away of the plant life. They live in the elements of air and light, and help man to be aware of the eternal transformation in the life of nature. Children and old people, as they are nearer to the dream world, are more open to their gracious gifts.

Philia, as the Being of Feeling, is especially aware of the power of the Sylphs to bring life and beauty into the world of nature. Their activity draws forth from human beings love for what the Sylphs are creating.

Astrid, as the Being of Thought, is more concerned with the contrast between growth and decline. She is aware of the strength-giving forces of the earth which stimulate new creativity and give joy to those who feel their power in bringing new life out of apparent death.

Luna, as the Being of Will, is most concerned with the shaping power within earth substance. Out of it clear cut forms are brought about. These inspire the will to strive for future activity.

We have heard in *The Guardian of the Threshold* how the Other Philia, through Johannes' progress, has become to him a helpful being. She is calling to him here to be aware of the magical power of the Sylphs to bring forth the blossom and awaken the hope that seeds will come to new life. He will then perhaps realise how in his own life past memories will arise and he will begin to understand the magical web of his own soul experiences. She leads him to recognise what he has brought about through his longing to dream into the hopes and wishes of his youth. He has here formed another spectral being, just as he had created his Double out of his unrecognised sensual attraction to Maria.

Rudolf Steiner has shown that we all bring with us into life a great burden of unredeemed Karma and normally this should gradually be transformed through our striving for higher knowledge. But in wishing to go back to the natural gifts of his early days and throw aside his later spiritual development, Johannes has failed to recognise this aspect of his past. Out of this failure Lucifer has been able to create a spectral form, 'The Spirit of Johannes' Youth', just as Ahriman called forth the Double owing to Johannes' repressed desires.

Lucifer, the Spirit of Johannes' Youth and Theodora now appear. The Spirit of Johannes' Youth appeals to him for help, for as long as Johannes is indulging youthful hopes and desires the Spirit is kept alive, but if he strives for higher wisdom then the Spirit will disappear. Lucifer reassures him that Johannes has longings that can never be satisfied through Maria's guidance, where he can achieve love, but only deprived of beauty. Lucifer will gradually enlighten Johannes and in the meantime will give his protection to the Spirit. If Johannes is concerned only with his own selfish personal development, the Spirit will be neglected and endure a shadow existence. But Lucifer will exert his age-old power to use Johannes' lack of self-knowledge and bring him to unite fully with the Spirit of his Youth.

The soul of Theodora, who guards Johannes, bends down in compassion over the Spirit of his Youth. She promises that if as a service to Johannes he will forego his own self-conscious life, she will bestow on him her feeling and unite him with the powers of the Elemental Spirits and thus he will be free from the enchantment of Lucifer. In reply to Lucifer's threat that Theodora cannot create beauty, she answers that there is a higher beauty born out of self-sacrifice.

As Theodora, Lucifer and the Spirit of Johannes' Youth disappear, the Other Philia again draws near to Johannes. There is one question he needs to demand of her, and that concerns the nature of the Spirit of his Youth. She shows him that he has created a half-wakened shadow Being and as long as he is not developing his further powers this will haunt him. Until he overcomes his infatuation with the past, this Being will be bound to him through his own guilt.

Johannes is grateful to the Other Philia for her guidance and realises the necessity of obeying her.

Scene Three
THE SAME SETTING AS SCENE TWO
Hilary and his three supporters, Bellicosus, Romanus and Torquatus, are discussing the difficulties presented by the Manager's determination to resign.

We see in this scene how difficult it is to bring new impulses into a concern that is firmly founded in agelong tradition. The problems aroused cause confusion in those striving for a solution and consequently little agreement can be found in their suggestions.

Romanus considers that the Manager's withdrawal is a sign that the time is not ready for Benedictus' pupils to bring their spiritual ideas into Hilary's workshops. Bellicosus would still like to think that the new impulse they received within the Temple should bring achievement, but he has his doubts about Capesius. Torquatus, too, has doubts about Capesius and points out that his withdrawal from his occult friends, is also a sign that the situation is not ripe for their venture. He adds also that the Manager has no confidence in Strader.

Romanus expresses his opinion that Strader is the only one capable of supporting the new work, as he is firmly grounded in practical life, while the others are in danger of falling into illusions once they try to bring their spiritual experiences into a realm with which they are not familiar.

At this moment, Ahriman passes across the stage behind the speakers. This is a sign that he is throwing his shadow across their counsel.

Bellicosus suggests that as Romanus has always been successful in every enterprise he has undertaken, the Manager may be convinced by him of Strader's real worth.

Romanus now makes a suggestion to Hilary. If he will undertake to work with Strader alone and decline the services of the other pupils of Benedictus, he himself will give all he has to support the enterprise. But Hilary is shocked at this suggestion and cannot believe it possible.

The four leave the stage. Capesius, Strader, Felix and Felicia Balde now approach. In this scene Capesius and Felix both show that they are again under the influence of Lucifer. They are more interested in their own spiritual development than they are in their relationship with others.

Capesius explains that owing to his vision into the soul of another, he realises he must give his full attention to his spiritual development, and not bring confusion through any outward enterprise.

Felix affirms that he has never felt so close to Capesius as at this moment. He tells Strader than one cannot attain true spiritual experience by striving for it. It will not come in answer to reason and any seeking makes it the more elusive.

Strader feels that Capesius and Felix are banishing him from their world. He needs to bring his spiritual striving into practical form in order to help others; he could face any opposition from the outside world without losing hope, but he cannot do without their help. He longs to enter their world.

Felix describes the mystic mood. It is to strive for naught, only to wait in peace and inward expectation. Any attempt to bring this mood into outer life destroys it. Capesius adds that he himself has had an experience because he was planning to enter into outer activity. He was granted a vision into the soul of another, but this revealed to him only the other's failure. He knew that this was a sign that he must withdraw from his plan to join with Hilary's enterprise.

Strader, however, feels that spirit light can illuminate him only when he devotes himself to thoughts of action. He longs to express spiritual truths in earthly form and bring light to human souls, who are striving to unite with the spirit world. He appeals to the World Spirit to show him whether this is error.

In response to his prayer, Strader receives his first visionary experience of his own inner being. He sees the confusion of his own thoughts between the ideas given to him by Benedictus and those of his everyday life as expressed by the Manager and inspired by Ahriman. The form of Benedictus appears before him and tells him that he must change his way of thinking. He must allow the reasoning power which he brings to the sense world and in which he has so much confidence now to lapse into a dream state, and on the other hand he must bring to life his own inner soul being of which he has never been fully conscious. Capesius and Felix have created an abyss between themselves and him but he must not complain; he should gaze into his abyss.

Ahriman now appears and mockingly comments that Benedictus cannot give him the right guidance. But Strader resolves to summon up his strength to gaze into the abyss. He beholds two phantom beings, wildly attacking each other; but the form of Maria comes to reproach him that owing to his lack of courage he is raying out fierce darkness and the phantoms that he beholds will display themselves in their true nature only when he learns to ray out light.

Ahriman now again sneeringly remarks that Maria's

wisdom is for Strader only foolishness. But Benedictus assures him that Maria has appeared to shelter him from beings of confusion who want to lead him only into the narrow realm of self. He tells Strader to look further into the abyss and watch the blue-reddish shadow that is approaching Felix and the reddish-yellow shade drawing near to Capesius. Their struggle is entirely different from his.

Ahriman again intervenes saying that although Benedictus means well he is incapable of seeing Strader's own phantoms as they are concealed behind him. Maria, however, encourages Strader by saying that the shades which Felix and Capesius have to transform are very different from those with which he has to wage his struggle, for his path must lead him to transform spiritual wisdom into deeds for earthly life.

Strader gradually awakens from his vision. Felix has observed that he has been wrapped in thought and now becomes a little apologetic. He says that he and Capesius do not want to drive him away, but only to persuade him of the true way to obtain spiritual vision. One cannot struggle to receive it or to force it into earthly service. It would be as though Felicia were trying to express her fairy stories in wooden puppets, which have no resemblance to her original imaginations.

At this point Felicia suddenly begins to show her sympathy with Strader. She accuses the other two of being so intent on developing mysticism that they are no longer interested in her fairy tales and she herself would love to see them brought to expression in artistic form and taken to give joy to children in their nurseries.

Scene Four
THE SAME LANDSCAPE
Romanus and the Manager are discussing Strader. Both

of them are aware of what is later confirmed by Benedictus, that Strader is inspired by certain supersensible Beings, but neither can judge of the nature of these. The Manager feels that they are demonic and will ruin any attempt to work with Hilary. Romanus considers that they are benign and that Strader has great gifts to bring to the future. What troubles the Manager is Strader's strongly compelling power, both in his speech and actions. Romanus acknowledges this and now shows a wonderful understanding of Strader's character.

Like Strader, Romanus has come through his own reasoning power to experience that reincarnation is the only answer to certain life problems. He has made a very close observation of Strader and from it has come to the conclusion that he must in a past life have acquired great faculties, far ahead of the people of his time.

We have here to remember that Simon the Jew was taken into the protection of the Knights Templar during their last stand, so that Romanus as the Grand Master of Ceremonies would have come strongly under his influence. Romanus now describes how many of the thoughts that came to him even in his younger days seem to him to have been given him by the Being of Strader. He is not afraid of undue influence; he feels he has found the right relationship, but acknowledges the very special gifts that Strader brings. All these ideas are very strange to the Manager and he needs time to consider them.

In conclusion Romanus repeats the words which Strader used at the end of Scene One: 'All that will come that has to come about'.*

---

*Collison's translation of this saying 'that which must will surely come to pass' is stronger and rather more easily understood.

Romanus' words begin to bring about a change in the Manager's ability to understand. As they go out, Johannes comes in thoughtfully and sits upon a rock. He is astonished that he has forgotten what he once knew so well, that it is possible for the spiritual striver at special moments to receive glimpses of the soul life of others. Long ago he had been able to read the thought processes of Capesius and Strader. Later he had realised Capesius' ability to understand, when he himself for the first time met his own Double. Then he also recognised his own close relationship with Capesius in a previous life. How was it that he had forgotten all this and how can he retain his knowledge for the future? From the distance comes the Double's reminder of the words of the Other Philia, who summoned Johannes to remember the enchanted weaving of his own being.

From now on, Johannes shows how his self-indulgence is leading him into continuous illusions. When the Double appears, he imagines it to be the Other Philia and asks to follow her. The Double would now seem to wish to awaken Johannes. He reproaches him for his guilt in leaving the Spirit of his Youth as a shadow while he himself is only anxious to live in his own youthful hopes. The Double cannot lead Johannes to the Spirit of his Youth but can only summon up a reflected image. This suddenly arouses Johannes to realise that it is his Double who has been guiding him. The Double then leads him to the Guardian of the Threshold.

The Guardian warns Johannes that while he is living in base desires he can experience only illusions. He cannot even know the Guardian in his true being while he lacks spirit peacefulness of soul. Johannes is commanded to call up the words of power that he knows, so that he may recognise the Guardian as he really is.

Here Ahriman appears as a mocker. He reproaches Johannes for being unable as an artist to create a more convincing picture of the Guardian. Johannes is thrown into utter confusion. Where can he find the truth? The Double calls upon him to ask himself. Aided by the Double's power, if he can in wakefulness gaze into that part of himself which is free from burning wishes, he will see the truth. Johannes repeats to himself the words of the Other Philia, and asks the enchanted weaving of his own being to reveal to him what is beyond his selfish wishes.

The thought forms of Benedictus and Maria appear. Maria warns him that while he lives in old worn out dreams he does not see her as she really is. Benedictus calls to him of the need to develop spirit peacefulness of soul. The appearance of Benedictus, Maria and the Guardian arouses Johannes to realise that he is still not seeing them truly. He ponders about the magical weaving of his own being, which will waken in him a memory of a long past experience which is throwing its shadow on the present scene.

As Johannes departs, Benedictus, Maria and Strader appear.

Strader is grateful that at the abyss of his own being Benedictus gives him helpful counsel, though he does not yet fully understand it. His whole intention is to give his strength to the plans of Hilary, but he realises that Capesius' support will no longer be there. Benedictus has to warn him that Johannes is also unready for the task and Maria will have for the present to accompany him. Strader now knows once more that he has to proceed in complete loneliness. Benedictus is led to inform him that there are certain supersensible beings who through Strader will become ripe to influence the world, but the time is not yet ready. If they were now to be active it would create evil. It is better for Strader that for the present he does not recognise them. Strader courageously declares that his loneliness will help him to forge the sword that is needed for his future development. The soul of Theodora appears to Strader and assures him that in the realms of light she will be with him to give him strength.

When Strader has retired, Maria expresses her surprise that Benedictus has spoken such fateful words. If Strader is not able to make use of them, will they not work ill for him and even be harmful for Benedictus himself?

Benedictus replies that he had been ordered by Destiny. The results will not be evil, although he cannot see how they will develop, because his vision of the future is clouded. Maria is astonished and asks what is disturbing his spiritual sight. Benedictus answers that it is the call of Johannes, who is in dire distress. In distant cosmic spaces in realms of frost, he is creating flames of fire, which are becoming active in Maria's own soul.

We learn later that a long past relationship between Johannes and Maria is the cause of the present disturbance. It is also awakening in Maria a memory of a critical turning point in her own spiritual life. It seems to her that her thinking is engaged in a fierce fight between flaming heat and waves of darkness, surrounded by cosmic fields of ice. It is her own thought, fighting with the power of Lucifer. Out of the struggle she feels that her own being is forcing its way into the light.

Scene Five
In the next two scenes we are granted a glimpse into the spiritual world experienced by the souls with whom we are concerned, between their past life and their present incarnation. In memory, looking back into their pre-earthly

life, they first see the scenes that are nearer to them in the Sun sphere, concerned with their descent to the earth, and only later do they see the Saturn sphere of the cosmic midnight. The Sun realm appears in a many-coloured radiance. To the right is Ahriman, and below him the Gnomes, and on the left Lucifer, with the Sylphs.

Souls are beginning to lose their memories of what they have passed through in the spiritual world and are becoming aware of their approach to the earth, which is indicated in the lower part of the scene. We see how Felix Balde and Capesius, who in their coming life are to be more connected with Lucifer, are here not fully prepared for entry into the weight and heaviness of earth. On the other hand, Strader and Hilary, who are anxious to achieve deeds for the good of humanity, are more under the spell of Ahriman.

The Soul Powers here offer guidance to Strader, to protect him from what might become a danger to him on earth.

Owing to his past life, Capesius is unable to see clearly in this realm. He is aware of the approach of a soul who, he feels, has much to bestow on him, but he cannot grasp who it is. Luna here gives him guidance. She shows that owing to the selfishness of his last life he needs to call up strength from a previous incarnation which he spent in earnest growth. Then he will be able to draw near to this soul who approaches him. Capesius wonders whether he owes a debt to this being, but Astrid now assures him that repayment will not be required in his coming life; this soul wishes to give strength to his thinking. The Other Philia warns him not to let the being exert too much power on him at this stage. We need to remember that the Other Philia is interested in developing the personal qualities of the souls which she influences.

Philia advises him that when in memory he goes back to the Saturn period of the cosmic midnight, if he remains awake he will realise that this being who is akin to him will bring him a sense for the meaning of life. We learn from the next scene that this being is Strader. He and Capesius are a wonderful complement to one another, Capesius living always in the world of ideas and Strader eager to become active in earthly life.

At this point Lucifer declares his intention of revealing worlds to the characters in the Sun realm which they are not strong enough themselves to face. Through the pain of their experience they will develop ego consciousness for their next life on earth.

Now Benedictus and Maria appear. Benedictus warns the souls that are present, they are making his sun-enlightened task more difficult because of their egoism with regard to their coming lives.

Maria wakens in them the memory that although during their last incarnation Benedictus was not on earth with them, nevertheless he had guided them in past lives. If they can now develop strength within them, they will be able to feel his continued benign presence.

Felix Balde and Capesius are aware of light-filled words sounding forth, but are not able to understand their meaning.

The soul of Felicia, who now appears, shows why Felix and Capesius are unable to comprehend the words of Benedictus and Maria. Felix is aware of the light but the words are only tones without meaning to him. Capesius can behold the stars but does not understand them.

Felicia's words, 'the script of the stars', awaken memories in Capesius of past times when his thoughts were full of glorious life, but now their being fades for him.

At the close of the scene the Guardian gives a stern warning to Felix and Capesius, who are under the influence of Lucifer. They are drawing near to other souls with whom they are connected, but they must on no account attempt to penetrate their thought life. Otherwise he would be obliged to separate them for countless ages.

Scene Six
THE SATURN SPHERE. The time of the cosmic midnight.

The soul of Capesius is becoming more aware of the one who was akin with him in a past life, but he cannot yet distinguish his real being. Together with Capesius appear the three characters who were with him as officials in the Templar Order, Romanus, Torquatus and Bellicosus. It is Romanus who reminds Capesius to awaken in his thoughts the picture of Simon the Jew, who had been admitted to their Order. As Capesius calls up vividly the image of Simon, another soul with whom he was connected in that period and who now awakens painful memories, draws near to him. Romanus tells him that this soul can be active only in the Sun sphere and must wander here in darkness. However, Capesius feels the presence of this newcomer is really burning him. He hears echoing back to him words that he spoke to Kean, Felix in his last incarnation, who had undertaken the care of the young daughter Capesius had deserted. Capesius, who feels the need to get to know this soul more intimately, now disappears from the scene.

At this moment the Other Philia leads in the souls of Theodora and Felicia. The soul of Torquatus here speaks of the influence he has exerted in the past over Felix to soften his tendency to become too stern, and to give him the gift of compassion. A gentle light is radiated from Theodora, who implores Felicia, with her loving power, to soothe Felix's solitude and awaken in him creative strength. Felicia declares herself willing to guide him until he can free himself from Lucifer's dominion and experience the light of the stars.

Theodora remembers how, in their past incarnations, she as Celia had a vision of her brother, Johannes, as Thomas the Miner, who had spoken a saying of the Templars, 'Out of the godhead rose the human soul. In death it can descend to depths of being. It will, in time, from death set free the spirit.' Her calling up of these words summons Lucifer, with the soul of Johannes, to the scene. The Other Philia undertakes to transform Theodora's noble sisterly love into soul power for the future. She then calls to Felicia to unite herself with the nature spirits of the stars, who will awaken in her the power of fantasy to inspire, in the future, human souls on earth. This refers to Felicia's special gift in the telling of fairy tales. Felix is slowly led away from the scene by Felicia, followed by Theodora. The soul of Romanus shows that the words of the Other Philia have aroused love and the impulse to action, to strengthen growth which will be needed in future lives on earth. Now Lucifer departs with the soul of Johannes.

The souls of Benedictus and Maria appear, together with the Guardian. The Guardian summons Benedictus and Maria to behold in the light of Saturn their cosmic midnight hour. Maria recalls here that in the Saturn sphere it is possible for those who are awake to receive flashes of vision which illuminate what is to happen in the next incarnation, but the lightning flash immediately disappears, although it has set a stamp upon future events. It is important to capture and retain truly, without illusion, what has been seen. Benedictus here speaks to Maria words which she later repeats to Johannes when urging him to learn to create anew when all seems to have been lost. Johannes is now in dire need of help. Maria is conscious of what is later to appear in her coming incarnation. At the end of Scene Four she experiences an intense soul struggle, and here in the Saturn sphere she is able to realise its true meaning. It is the fight of her own thinking power with the might of Lucifer, which in earthly life causes her to make her solemn earnest vow to save Johannes.

Lucifer now proclaims his own fiery force. He states that in the future Maria will have to change her way of dealing with Johannes, who is under his power.

Johannes is aware of souls, but cannot call up the strength to recognise what is happening around him. Philia summons him to behold what is illuminated in the lightning flash of the cosmic midnight. Johannes now becomes aware of the presence of Benedictus and Maria. He realises that Maria, who is so near and dear to him, will be able to ray into his being the words of Benedictus. Benedictus calls to Maria to strengthen her will so that when on earth, her words will radiate into her friend's soul. Maria summons up in herself the great love she feels for Benedictus, who has guided her so often in past lives through every trial. She forms a word which shall sound into Johannes' soul as a tone which will awaken in him in their following life on earth so that they may come together in harmony. She asks of eternity that it may preserve the blessing of their union with their great leader.

As Maria has glimpsed what is revealed by the lightning flash it now fades and the thunder sinks into silence. The Guardian summons Astrid to preserve this experience of Maria and bring it to her in her life on earth. He shows that another memory will now awaken in Maria of a long past incarnation, in which she failed. Although a soul should

never wish to fall, it can from failure acquire great strength.
Maria feels the blissfulness of the starry world and in this mood will live together with the soul of the one she loves. Luna now undertakes to preserve her achievement in this realm so that it may ripen into deeds on earth.

Johannes recognises the presence of Maria as a star which glows with gentle light. He then realises the approach of another star, which is the Spirit of his Youth. The Spirit of Johannes' Youth promises to give inspiration to Johannes in his next life, but implore him not to neglect him or he will have to live as a shadow among the shades.

Lucifer assures the Spirit, as he later reaffirms on earth, that he reads in Johannes' soul longings that will not be satisfied by those who cultivate a higher love deprived of beauty.

Scene Seven
The next two scenes present a view of an initiation in the time of the ancient Egyptian civilisation. The human being at that stage had not developed ego consciousness and consequently the Neophyte was led through the necessary experiences under the complete control of a number of initiates. These scenes give us clues leading to an understanding of the difficulties endured by Capesius, Maria, Johannes and Hilary in the early scenes of the present drama.

In the seventh scene the Hierophant (Capesius), who is responsible for the preparations of the holy rite, is consulting with his helpers, the Warden of the Temple (Felix) and the Mystic (Felicia). He is concerned about the condition of the young priest, the former incarnation of Maria, who is to be initiated, and he enquires about what they know of his state of development, as he is to become a counsellor of the Pharaoh. The Mystic replies that he is often observed to be in spirit trance and therefore would probably be more suited to serve the Temple than the Court.

After the Mystic's departure the Hierophant confides further in the Warden, upon whose seership he has often relied. We here see the origin of Capesius' reliance on the spiritual wisdom of Felix in their later incarnations. He asks for the Warden's support, because he knows that the Neophyte has many earthly longings and unredeemed desires. He is not condemning the priest, but he is condemning an initiation which impresses into the young soul all its thoughts and feelings with no regard for any personal qualities. He realises that the sacred rites have a great spiritual meaning and any infringement will bring not only disaster on those who perform the ceremony, but will also have effect in the spiritual world.

After the departure of the Warden, the Hierophant gives further expression to his own doubts. He feels that the time has come when it is no longer right to lead a young neophyte like a victim to an initiation of which he is fully unconscious. But he cannot discuss this with the Chief Hierophant of all, who is vowed to silence. None of the speaker's collaborators has any understanding of the meaning of the ritual, and he feels an intense solitude. We see here the origin of Capesius' great loneliness in his spiritual life. As Hierophant he appeals to the heavens for illumination, but receives no response.

Scene Eight
Before the curtains open to disclose the scene of the Temple where the initiation is to take place, we see a woman lying at the gates. This is a former incarnation of Johannes/Thomasius. She is in love with the young priest who is to be

initiated, and she knows that he will now have to renounce all earthly ties. In her despair she longs to take part in his initiation. She thinks if she concentrates all her thoughts and feelings on what is happening within, she may be granted a share of his experiences.

The curtains unclose, revealing the central altar, behind which stands the Chief Hierophant, a former incarnation of Benedictus. To the right and left are two Sphinxes, similar in form to the one which can now be seen near the Great Pyramid at Gizeh. These represent Lucifer and Ahriman, who in that ancient time had little access to the human soul. It was only after the development of ego consciousness when man became interested on the one hand in his sense impressions and therefore under the power of Ahriman, and on the other absorbed in his own feeling life and hence open to the allurements of Lucifer, that these Beings had very much power.

In this scene are gathered together practically all the characters who have appeared during the four dramas. In the early initiations it was important for the Neophyte to be guided by twelve initiates, representative of the twelve different points of view.

The Neophyte is led in by the Warden and the Mystic, and is first of all brought to experience the Real Beings which are active behind the work of the four elements. We find here these elements are represented by Strader and the three characters who were present with Hilary in the Rosicrucian Brotherhood.

The one to be initiated needs to realise that Earth, Air, Fire and Water are all present within his own being; but in everyday life he can experience them only through his physical body, and therefore is unaware of their real power and meaning.

The Temple Warden instructs the Neophyte that in physical life and within himself all he can come to know is illusion. He is to be raised to a vision of the Spiritual Powers which have created this world of semblance. He is led to be aware of the real nature of Earth and Air. Then to lead him to an understanding of Fire and Water the Chief Hierophant commands him to gaze into the flame on the altar. This leaps up then more vividly. When the Neophyte has experienced this, the Chief Hierophant calls upon the Hierophant to explore the soul that is to be initiated. It is the task of the Hierophant to instil into the Neophyte the thoughts and feelings which are required, but he withholds this influence, and now the Neophyte, having described his bliss at the visions of the spirit world, expresses his longing to return into the pleasures of sense existence.

All except the Hierophant are horrified, and the Chief Hierophant declares that earthly desires have been offered to the Spiritual World and this is sacrilege. The Recorder, a previous incarnation of Hilary, attacks the Hierophant, since this sacrilege could never have occurred if he had performed his true priestly duty. The Hierophant explains that he has obeyed Divine guidance, for the time has come when the individual being should become free of the group ego. Hence he did not instil into the Neophyte the instruction which ritual required. The youth's future destiny will show what he is capable of achieving. Those present demand atonement for this sacrilege.

At this moment the Sphinxes, which have hitherto always been silent, begin to speak. This is experienced only by the Chief Hierophant, the Hierophant and the Neophyte. The Sphinx representing Ahriman claims that he will capture for his own realm what has happened in this sacred rite and will develop it for future power. Lucifer declares that he will take hold of what here has appeared as desires and will in future transform beauty into reality.

The Chief Hierophant realises that the time has come in which spirit can speak through matter. Destiny has enabled the cosmic word to resound. The Hierophant adds that the rites they perform are not for themselves alone, but that world events are expressed through them.

In this scene we recognise how the opposition of Hilary as the Recorder to the Hierophant (Capesius) influences his present life on earth. As the Grand Master of the Rosicrucian Brotherhood he was unable to recognise the Being of Ahriman when he and Romanus entered Ahriman's kingdom. This is shown in *The Portal of Initiation*. Later he had difficulty in transforming the business concern of his family to one which would express the ideals of the group around Benedictus. In particular he had doubts about Capesius.

Here also is illustrated the origin of Johannes' longing to live in the dreams of his youth, created when, as the woman outside the Temple, his burning desires followed the Hierophant through the initiation ceremony.

Scene Nine
A ROOM IN HILARY'S HOUSE suitable for study.
While Maria is alone in meditation she is aware of the approach of Astrid, whom in the past she has always known as a shadow being, but now recognises as a shining spirit form. Astrid recalls the memory of the cosmic midnight and brings back to her the words she spoke when she entreated Eternity to allow her to live together in peace with her leader and the soul she loves. These words stir memories within Maria and she asks for strength that

she does not lose her experiences when she becomes fully awake in earthly life. Luna appears, to give her the forces of will and reminds her of the saying of the Guardian, that a soul should never wish itself to fall, but when it does it must learn through its failures.

Gradually forms begin to appear to Maria, and she sees the picture of a youthful mystic before a sacred flame and the stern words of the Highest Hierophant calling to him to read what is revealed within the fire. She is then aware of the horror of the gathered mystics at the Neophyte's confession of his own desires. At this moment the Guardian appears and recalls the words of the Highest Hierophant. As Maria remembers this command, Benedictus appears, for her memory of his words has called him to her. He reminds her that when he appealed to her in that long past age, she was not ready to follow him, but what had been stored within her soul awakened in later lives, so that she became his earnest pupil. He then quotes the saying of the Hierophant, Capesius, that the mystic ceremony in ancient Egypt was not for themselves alone. This awakens in Maria the memory of the Hierophant, who had not guided her in the accepted way because unconsciously he bore within himself a premonition of the radiant light that was to dawn in Greece, when man began to awake to self-consciousness. She also becomes aware of his feeling of solitude in the stern spirit shrine.

Benedictus explains that this feeling of loneliness was a seed which bore fruit in Capesius' later lives and has now driven him to wish to follow Felix.

Maria wonders how she can find again the woman who was clinging to the gates of the Temple. The Guardian appears and tells her to seek for the one who is struggling to free himself from his creation of a soul shadow who is now condemned to a life of shades. Maria feels the light of calm and peacefulness that rays from the Guardian and which gives her strength. She is grateful to these Spirit Stars, the Guardian, Astrid and Luna, who have given her the power to grasp what happened at the cosmic midnight.

Scene Ten
THE SAME AS SCENE NINE
Johannes is sitting in thought. A picture appears before him of the woman at the entrance to the Temple in the Egyptian scene, which holds him spellbound, though he cannot call up any definite feeling with regard to it. Nevertheless he is strengthened by what he beholds, and wishes to know its meaning. He hears, as though at a distance, the words of the Other Philia 'The enchanted weaving of your own Being'. She then appears to him and tells him he must seek within himself in order to free the shadow being which he has created. He must try to penetrate the scene which has been preserved for him in spirit light. Then he will realise what he will need to do in his next life to redeem his guilt. When he seeks for guidance she says that she is also part of his own inner being. She is the feeling of love within him, and if he would entrust himself to her he would gradually find the meaning of the picture he has seen.

Johannes becomes aware of a shining spirit star approaching him. Gradually forms appear, and he sees the Neophyte standing before the sacred flame and hears the words of the Highest Hierophant. A vision now appears before the Neophyte of the woman at the Temple gates.

Maria now comes before him. She tells him that if he wishes to free himself from his confusion he must ponder more fully this picture to understand it rightly. He must follow the indications of the woman who is pointing out the way through her service to the dim shadow which now haunts him.

At this moment the Spirit of Johannes' Youth appears. He says that he will be for ever rightly connected with Johannes if the latter lovingly retains the power which the youthful Neophyte has faithfully preserved for him through the ages. Johannes must now recognise in truth the spirit of Maria who stands beside him.

Maria reminds Johannes that he has been wishing to see her in a form that is not her true being. But her holy earnest vow is raying forth strength so that he may retain what he has already gained in the past. She no longer speaks to him of creating out of the empty fields of ice, but tells him that he will behold her in the bright realms of light, where beauty can awaken powers of life. He must seek her in the grounds of world where souls must struggle in love to find the gods and so in the All learn to understand the Self.

There now comes a re-echo of what happened at the end of Scene Three in *The Guardian of the Threshold*. Lucifer appears and summons all his compelling powers to take possession of Johannes' being, so that he may be fully captured for Lucifer's domain.

At this moment Benedictus comes upon the scene and warns that Maria's holy earnest vow rays forth light so that in future Johannes will admire Lucifer yet will not fall. Lucifer once more declares that he will fight, but Benedictus states that in fighting he will serve the gods.

Scene Eleven
THE SAME AS SCENE TEN Benedictus and Strader together.

Strader is recalling the vision which he saw when he stood

at his soul's abyss, as described towards the end of Scene Three. He is pained that Maria spoke to him so harshly, warning him that he was raying out darkness owing to his cowardice. Benedictus tells Strader that this picture is not complete reality. The Spirit is trying to lead him to a new stage of development and he has himself formed this into the image of Maria. He now needs to strengthen his soul forces to understand his picture truly. There are different stages of courage, and what at one level can be bravery can cease to be so at another.

We can understand this if we realise that it is possible to work with great courage to achieve certain earthly aims, but at a further stage of development we can see that this was of little value. To be faithful to a spiritual ideal when none around are able to understand it requires quite a different approach and to hold on to one's former type of courage is merely clinging to traditional ways of behaviour.

Strader is very much disheartened, because Romanus has tried to separate him from Benedictus and his pupils, and he feels that if there is no opportunity for him to carry out the ideals for which he has so long striven, then his life becomes meaningless. He wonders if he is able to develop the strength of which Benedictus speaks, because this struggle is sapping his life forces. Benedictus encourages him by saying that Maria and Johannes have now come a great step forward in seership, and will be able to unite their strength with his for future spiritual aims. Collison's translation is here easier to follow than that of Hans Pusch. Benedictus explains that occult truths give not guidance but creative strength. He then quotes the words that Strader has come to recognise, 'all that will come that has to come about', which also ring more powerfully in the original translation, as 'all that must will surely come to pass'.

However, Strader is still troubled about his relationship with Romanus and tells Benedictus of another vision he has recently had. It seems to him that under the guidance of Benedictus he is steering a boat, conveying Maria and Johannes to a sphere of work, when another vessel containing Romanus and Hilary's Manager attack them. There is a fierce fight, in which Ahriman comes to the aid of Romanus and the Manager, and Strader finds himself engaged in battling with Ahriman. Then Theodora comes to his aid. Benedictus tells Strader that this picture is not yet truly formed, but as he strengthens his soul powers he will see it differently.

Scene Twelve
AHRIMAN'S ROCKY KINGDOM

Flames appear from above, expressing all the pressure brought upon Ahriman by Benedictus and his circle.

Ahriman is aware that he has lost an opportunity of influencing Maria and Johannes, for they have learned to recognise Lucifer. His only method now of gaining a hold over Benedictus's pupils is through Strader. Although the latter has heard a great deal of the teaching of Benedictus and has even been sent half-conscious into Ahriman's kingdom, there is a great hope that he will forget these experiences, because he has no true understanding of the world of nature. Strader imagines that all natural forces are of material origin, and does not recognise that Ahriman's spiritual interference blinds men's vision. Ahriman feels the need of becoming more active to gain control over Strader, and plans to call in the help of Ferdinand Fox, who he thinks is clever and shrewd enough in everyday life to be able to influence Strader.

The soul of Ferdinand Fox is led in blindfold, as he is not conscious that he is in Ahriman's kingdom, but he will receive Ahriman's suggestions and they will inspire him in his waking life.

When Ahriman questions Fox about his knowledge of Strader, Fox speaks very contemptuously about the mystic snobs with whom Strader is now connected. Ahriman can read in the Book of Fate that Strader's life is drawing to a close. Benedictus is not aware of this, for even initiates are not able to tell the hour of death. Ahriman knows that he must get hold of Strader while he is on earth, for after death he will belong to Benedictus' circle. He considers that the one way in which Fox can effectively impress Strader will be through his shrewdness in understanding material processes. He suggests to Fox that he should persuade Strader that his invention is faulty. This is exactly what Fox himself has been inclined to do, and he feels that he will be able to show Strader that his invention is a failure not only in detail but in its whole design.

After Fox's departure, Ahriman confesses that the power of Benedictus and his pupils is burning him, so he must act quickly. The soul of Theodora appears, and tells him that however hard he tries to force himself on Strader, she is at his side. Ahriman realises that if Strader remembers her, the battle will be lost, but he lives in hope that he will forget her.

Scene Thirteen
A LARGE RECEPTION ROOM IN HILARY'S HOUSE
where Hilary and Romanus are in conversation. Hilary is lamenting to Romanus that he is almost crushed by the failure of his plans. Benedictus and his circle have withdrawn and the Manager is intending to desert him. Hilary

has always longed to accomplish perfect deeds, but has never attained the right thoughts from which they could spring. He is aware that Ferdinand Fox is sowing serious doubts of Strader's whole plan, and he himself is now disillusioned.

Hilary's desire to perform perfect deeds shows that he is really trying to cling to the past. In our present incarnation we can perform only imperfect deeds, which are as seeds for the future.

Romanus now repeats the warning he gave to Hilary in Scene Eight of *The Guardian of the Threshold*, where the two of them enter Ahriman's kingdom. He has often found that Hilary's spiritual vision is seriously at fault and this leads him into delusions, which weigh on Romanus' soul as a kind of nightmare. Hilary's first understanding of Strader was correct, but he is now led into a completely mistaken judgment. Even if Ferdinand Fox has found faults in Strader's design, the latter will learn through his mistakes and courageously go ahead, for it is through facing mistakes that one comes to the truth. The one who is not afraid of failure will always ultimately succeed. He sees Strader going forward undaunted and reaching the Threshold, where he will meet with the Guardian.

Romanus here again shows a wonderful understanding of Strader, which we can relate to their relationship in the Egyptian Temple scene where Strader represented the Fire element and Romanus that of the Earth. Fire and Earth are both expressions of will.

Hilary has heard before similar words to those used now by Romanus but never before did he really understand them. He is also now awakening to a new vision.

Hilary and Romanus leave the stage, and the Secretary shows in Capesius and Felix Balde. They have come to see

Benedictus, but as he has not yet returned from a journey they have asked to speak with Hilary instead. The Secretary goes in quest of Hilary.

Capesius has had an interesting experience. Early in the morning, while he was resting in a mystic mood, he became aware of Strader standing beside him, and at first Strader repeated the words which Felix Balde had spoken to him towards the end of Scene Three, when he and Capesius had refused to unite with Hilary's plans. At that time he warned Strader that by entering earthly deeds he would lose the power of attaining spirit vision. Strader was now repeating the words of Felix Balde, 'To strive for nothing ... wait in peaceful stillness, one's inmost being filled with expectation... that is the mystic mood.' But then Strader adds that if one meditates rightly then the right thoughts can come in daily life and even give one guidance in moments of action. Felix Balde says that these words are like an echo of his own, repeated by Strader, but somewhat misunderstood. However, Capesius shows that they are really quite different and he continues to add Strader's further words. The one who seeks only a mystic mood tends to weave a dark veil through his ecstatic life of feeling, and falls into illusions.

Felix considers that this is a complete misinterpretation of his own meaning, which is leading Capesius into error.

At this moment Philia appears, but is understood only by Capesius. She tells him that if he will attend to what has come to him unsought, it will bring enlightenment and strengthen him. To his own Sun-filled being the light of Saturn will radiate wisdom so that he will comprehend what he can know as earthly man. Then she will be able to lead him to the Guardian.

Felix Balde has been aware of the sound of words, but

he cannot make any sense of them. Capesius learned from Strader the need to bring his spirit wisdom down into earthly life, but Felix Balde is still determined to keep to his own way of mystic experience, and therefore cannot follow what Philia has to say.

To understand this incident fully, we need to know what is to happen at the end of the following scene, where we learn of Strader's death. Now that he has overcome his earthbound thinking and has entered the spiritual world, he is able to ray down light on his comrades. We can perhaps relate Felix Balde's inability here to comprehend what Capesius has received, by considering the time of the Egyptian incarnation. When the Hierophant (Capesius) described to the Warden (Felix Balde) his realisation that a new age was dawning through the gradual approach of ego consciousness, the Warden showed no interest or understanding in these views.

Scene Fourteen
THE SAME ROOM AS IN SCENE THIRTEEN
Hilary's wife is deeply distressed by the difficulties which have assailed Hilary's plans and she is trying to persuade the Manager not to desert her husband. But he considers that it would be against his principles to serve a concern which is run on ideas which he cannot approve. However, he acknowledges that he has been very much impressed by the forceful way in which Romanus spoke of Strader, and this has stirred him to wish to understand something of the spirit. Hilary's wife reproaches him for considering only Romanus' views of Strader. We can understand this contrast only if we realise that Strader is no longer present on earth. Romanus had been describing Strader's struggles and his courage to learn through failure, whereas

Hilary's wife, like Capesius, has received a ray of inspiration from Strader, who has now won through his earthly difficulties, though at the expense of his life. She is thus aware of his enlightenment and his relationship with Theodora.

At this moment the Secretary comes in and reports the news of Strader's death. Hilary's wife hurries out to console her husband and the Manager is left alone. The shock of this news makes him aware of the poverty of his own soul life. Without his conscious intention he finds that he has been swept into the tangled web of destiny involving Hilary and his circle. He recalls the words used by Strader, 'that will come which has to come about', and these now seem to him to have been inspired from the spirit world, and whatever happens he feels that he must learn to understand them. The death of Strader has awakened him to a new consciousness.

Scene Fifteen
THE SAME ROOM
The Other Maria, whom we met in *The Portal of Initiation* has now been the Nurse of Dr. Strader in his last illness. She brings a message for Benedictus and while she waits for him she and the Secretary speak of Strader. The Secretary is chiefly impressed by Strader's breadth of understanding; how he never spoke of his ideals until he had viewed them from every possible standpoint and had seen their reality. The Nurse adds too a picture of Strader's character which perhaps we had not yet very much associated with him. She describes how he was activated always by his need for love. Apart from his seven years of bliss with Theodora, his life had been one of loneliness, and although the mystics had shared their thoughts with him, his great need was through love to fulfil his earthly deeds. Hence even in his

last illness he was absorbed in thoughts of his task. They both agree that Theodora was his active inspiration and she was with him at the last. The Nurse realises that earthly life is full of riddles, but Sun-Beings such as Strader help to light the path of those around them as the sun illuminates the planets.

When Benedictus enters, the Secretary retires and the Nurse delivers a letter from Strader containing his last words to his spirit leader. Benedictus questions her about Strader's closing hours and she describes how for some time he lived with thoughts of his work, but then Theodora came nearer to him and he gently renounced his earthly striving and passed peacefully into the spirit world. Benedictus thanks the Nurse for her devoted care.

In his letter, Strader describes how he had continued to strengthen his own soul powers and thus came to realise that the hindrances to his work arose not from outer circumstances, but from his own erroneous thinking. Then the picture he described to Benedictus changed, and instead of Ahriman as the ally of Romanus and the Manager, he saw a spirit messenger, representative of his own thought being. At that moment Benedictus realises that the last words of the letter have become illegible, and suddenly Ahriman appears.

Ahriman claims to bring Benedictus further knowledge of the Being of Strader. As he is not yet fully recognised, he feels he may achieve some end. Benedictus replies that he and his followers will always be aware of Strader's presence and demands that Ahriman makes himself more clearly known. Ahriman states that as Benedictus' aim is for self-knowledge, surely he is willing to accept whatever a spirit visitor is willing to give him. However, Benedictus replies that what he gives can be of value only if it is selfless.

In describing Strader he must be able to live into the understanding of the one to whom he is speaking, so that together they may be able to create a truer spiritual picture of the one who has passed over.

Ahriman realises that in a moment he will be recognised, and the power of Benedictus will work to destroy him, so he turns away.

Benedictus now knows it has been Ahriman who approached him. His words imply that Ahriman has been allowed the use of power in order to tempt man, so that man may develop his own ego forces. Ahriman imagines that the use of his power to gain a kingdom of his own will bring him happiness; but on the contrary, as we have observed from the scenes of Ahriman's kingdom, his quest brings him only disappointment and acute pain. He does not see that in the distant future he will be redeemed. His aim has been to confuse men's thinking, to get power over them, but when he realises that he should unite with their spiritual thought then redemption will come. He appears to men in a disguised form, in order to mislead them, and has hoped that through Strader he could gain control over the circle of Benedictus. In the future, Benedictus' disciples will be able to recognise him in all his different appearances.

Benedictus now speaks of the victory of Strader, who has put Ahriman to flight and thus attained his full Sun-filled power. He will now be able to pour down light upon the mystic circle and give new strength to Maria and Johannes for their future work, so that their enlightened spirit thinking may recognise Ahriman in all his disguises and will no longer be led astray.

It may seem strange to the reader, or to the one who sees the play performed for the first time, that at the end

Benedictus is left alone upon the stage. But we have to remember that a fifth drama was being planned. However, owing to the outbreak of war and the new activities following its conclusion, this was never developed. Nevertheless, the final words descriptive of Strader do contain a very strong impression of the power he will now be able to ray down upon the followers of Benedictus, and of the overcoming of Ahriman's might, as well as the latter's final redemption.

We have also to realise that through the memory of their Egyptian incarnation, Maria and Johannes are now free, and Capesius, through Strader's influence, has again won a victory over his longing to retire into the mystic mood.

LECTURES BY RUDOLF STEINER USEFUL AS BACKGROUND READING TO THE MYSTERY DRAMAS

From Jesus to Christ, ten lectures, Karlsruhe (5-14 October 1911): see lectures two, seven and nine. Rudolf Steiner Press, London 1973.
Genesis, ten lectures, Munich (17-26 August 1910): see lectures one and six. Rudolf Steiner Press, London 1982.
Gospel of St Matthew, twelve lectures, Berne (1-12 September 1910): see lectures five, ten and twelve. Rudolf Steiner Press, London 1982.
Influences of Lucifer and Ahriman, five lectures, Dornach and Berne (1, 2, 4, 9, 15 November 1919) which throws further light on these beings. Steiner Book Centre, Canada.
Interpretation of Fairy Tales, one lecture, Berlin (26 December 1908). A guide to the wisdom in fairy tales. Rudolf Steiner Press, London. New edition in preparation.
Mission of Individual Folk Souls, eleven lectures, Christiania (Oslo) (7-17 June 1910). See chapter ten. Rudolf Steiner describes the Hibernian Mysteries as the oldest of the Post-Atlantean Mysteries. They were established before the destruction of Atlantis, and from them streamed the wisdom that inspired the Indian and later civilisations.
Also *Mystery Knowledge and Mystery Centres*, fourteen lectures, Dornach (23 November – 23 December 1923). Both published by Rudolf Steiner Press, London.
Road to Self-Knowledge and the Threshold of the Spiritual World, see lecture five (especially in relation to Baldes and Capesius) and lecture seven (information on Johannes), both contained in 'Threshold' section. Rudolf Steiner Press, London 1975.

Cosmic and Human Metamorphosis, seven lectures, Berlin (6 February — 20 March 1917): see lecture entitled *Errors and Truths*, Rudolf Steiner Press, London.

Secrets of the Threshold, eight lectures, Munich (24-31 August 1913), for details of Lucifer and Ahriman see lecture two. The first half of lecture five for a study of Professor Capesius, and the first half of lecture seven for information about the character of Johannes and the 'Double'. Rudolf Steiner Press, London.

BIBLIOGRAPHY

Commentary on Rudolf Steiner's Four Mystery Plays, H. Collison, Rudolf Steiner Publishing Co., 1949.
Four Mystery Dramas, translated H. Pusch, 2nd ed., Steiner Book Centre, Canada, 1978.
Four Mystery Plays, translated A. Bittleston, 1st ed., Rudolf Steiner Press, London 1983.
Green Snake and the Beautiful Lily, J. von Goethe, translated T. Carlyle, Floris Books.
Three Lectures on the Mystery Dramas, Rudolf Steiner, Basel (17 September 1910), Berlin (31 October 1910 and 9 December 1911). Anthroposophic Press, New York.
Working Together on Rudolf Steiner's Mystery Dramas, H. Pusch, 1st ed., Anthroposophic Press, 1980.